HOMENAJE A WALT WHITMAN / HOMAGE TO WALT WHITMAN

PS

JAÉN, Didier Tisdel, comp. and tr. Homage to Walt Whitman; a Collection of Poems from the Spanish. bilingual ed. Alabama, 1969. 87p 69-16161. 5.00

CHOICE   FEB. '70
Language & Literature
Romance

Jaén presents a selection of nine poems dedicated to Whitman by various Spanish and Spanish-American authors, as well as a commentary on each poet, and a new translation of José Martí's essay on Whitman. The translations are all good, sometimes excellent, and the selection, although small, is admirable, avoiding minor poems of scant value. The foreword, a short essay by Jorge Luis Borges, provides contemporary perspective particularly valuable due to the undeniable talent and insight of this extraordinary Argentinian writer. Recommended for students of Whitman of Hispanic poetry, and of Spanish stylistics and translation.

HOMENAJE A WALT WHITMAN

HOMAGE TO WALT WHITMAN

A Collection of Poems from the Spanish

Translated and Annotated by
Didier Tisdel Jaén

Foreword by
Jorge Luis Borges

UNIVERSITY OF ALABAMA PRESS

UNIVERSITY, ALABAMA

Copyright © 1969 by
UNIVERSITY OF ALABAMA PRESS

Standard Book Number: 8173–7600–3
Library of Congress Catalog Card Number: 69–16161

Manufactured in the United States of America
Designed by Robert L. Nance

ACKNOWLEDGMENTS

To THE MANY FRIENDS who amiably and enthusiastically answered my constant queries in regard to words, phrases, rhythm, and nuances of language, I am deeply grateful and I only regret that I cannot list all of them. In particular, I wish to express my gratitude to William Burford, of the University of Montana, to Eloise Roach, of the University of Texas, and to Timothy Campbell and Carl Stanley Ferguson, for reading all or part of the manuscript and offering invaluable suggestions and commentaries that significantly helped to improve its final version. This in no way implies that they are to share in the blame for any imperfections that may still remain in it, since I had the final word, and, therefore, I must be held responsible for these.

I am also indebted to the following authors and publishers who have graciously conceded permission to use the copyrighted works here presented: Jorge Luis Borges, to whom I am doubly grateful for the poem *Camden, 1892* and for the Foreword written expressly for the present volume; to León Felipe, for the excerpt from the introduction to his Spanish translation of *Leaves of Grass* (may the brief poem included here serve as well as a homage to the memory of this Spanish poet who died in

ACKNOWLEDGMENTS

Mexico in October, 1968); to Editorial Sudamericana, S.A., Buenos Aires, for the poem by Ezequiel Martínez Estrada; to Cuadernos Americanos and Alfredo Cardona Peña for the *Lectura de Walt Whitman;* to New Directions Publishing Corporation for the *Oda a Walt Whitman,* by Federico García Lorca; to Pedro Mir for his *Contracanto a Walt Whitman: Canto a nostros mismos;* and to Pablo Neruda for his *Oda a Walt Whitman.*

My sincere thanks also to the University of California, Davis, for a grant to aid in the preparation of the collection.

CONTENTS

CONTENTS

PREFACE

WALT WHITMAN was first introduced to the Spanish literary world by the Cuban writer and patriot José Martí, who lived in New York from 1880 to 1895. While devoting himself to the cause of Cuban liberation from Spain, laying the ground work for the revolution, and, finally, giving his own life at the outbreak of the war in a skirmish with Spanish forces on the island in 1895, Martí managed to carry on a prolific journalistic activity, contributing articles on the United States and the American scene in general to several Spanish American newspapers

His article on the North American poet, published in 1887 in *El Partido Liberal*, of Mexico City, and in *La Nación*, of Buenos Aires,[1] received immediate notice among Spanish literary circles on both sides of the Atlantic, as revealed by two of the most important Spanish-

[1] "El Poeta Walt Whitman," in *Obras completas* (La Habana: Editorial Nacional de Cuba, 1964), vol. XIII, pp. 129–43. Translated by Juan de Onís in *The America of José Martí* (New York: The Noonday Press, 1953), pp 239–58; by Arnold Chapman in *Walt Whitman Abroad*, ed. Gay Wilson Allen (Syracuse: Syracuse University Press, 1955), pp. 201–13; and by Luis A. Baralt in *Martí on the U.S.A.* (Carbondale: Southern Illinois University Press, 1966), pp. 3–16. See also Appendix I, in this volume.

language poets of the twentieth century. The Nicaraguan Rubén Darío, father of modern Spanish poetry and author of a sonnet to Walt Whitman, credited Martí with introducing to Spanish readers the image of

> a patriarchal, pre-eminent and lyrically majestic Walt Whitman, before—long before—France became acquainted, through Sarrazin, with the Biblical author of *Leaves of Grass*.[2]

And the Spaniard Juan Ramón Jiménez gave similar credit to Martí:

> Whitman, more American than Poe, came to all of us Spaniards, I think, through Martí. His essay on Whitman, which, I am sure, inspired Darío's sonnet to the "good old man," in *Azul*, was the first knowledge I had about the dynamic and delicate poet of "Autumn Rivulets."[3]

Since then, Walt Whitman has held a special place in the Spanish literary world, particularly in Spanish America.[4] He is, of course, the poet of America and Democracy, but his lyrical tone, hinted at by Juan Ramón Jiménez, has not escaped notice among Spanish critics and poets. Miguel de Unamuno, in an essay titled "Adamic Song,"[5] exalted Walt Whitman's ennumerative style as an expression of pure, unadorned lyricism; and Jorge Luis Borges, with his rare perception of literature, has written a couple

[2] Translation of a passage from *Los raros*, in *Obras completas* (Madrid: A. Aguado, 1950), vol. II, p. 486.

[3] Translation of a passage from *Españoles de tres mundos* (Buenos Aires: Losada, 1942), p. 33.

[4] The main study on the subject is the book by Fernando Alegría, *Walt Whitman en Hispanoamérica* (Mexico: Studium, 1964). See also John E. Englekirk, "Notes on Whitman in Spanish America," *Hispanic Review*, vol. VI (1938), pp. 133–38; and "Walt Whitman y el anti-modernismo," *De lo nuestro y lo ajeno* (Pittsburgh: Biblioteca del Nuevo Mundo), vol. IV.

[5] Translated by Fernando Alegría in *Walt Whitman Abroad*, pp. 220–23. Spanish text, "El canto adánico," in *El espejo de la muerte*, in *Obras completas* (Madrid: A. Aguado, 1958), vol. II, p. 763. Originally published in *Los lunes de El Imparcial* (Madrid, 1906).

PREFACE

of penetrating essays calling attention to the lyrical as well as other aspects of Walt Whitman's poetry.[6]

In the present volume, I have selected and translated some of the poetic homages Spanish-language poets have rendered to Walt Whitman,[7] proclaiming him one of the greatest poets of humanity. But these poems were not written only to Walt Whitman the poet. For Walt Whitman is also many other things: a comrade, a friend, Democracy and America, a tragic hero, and human brotherhood. I do not mean that he is merely a symbol of these things. In a sense, he *is* these things, and these poems are written to celebrate them. Walt Whitman is one of the names they have.

Didier Tisdel Jaén

Davis, California
January 1, 1969

---

[6] "El otro Whitman," dated 1929, in *Discusión* (Buenos Aires and Barcelona: M. Gleizer, 1932), pp. 65–70, and "Nota sobre Whitman," in *Otras inquisiciones, 1937–1952* (Buenos Aires: Sur, 1952), pp. 81–87. The latter in translation by Ruth L. C. Simms, *Other Inquisitions, 1937–1952* (Austin: University of Texas Press, 1965), paperback edition by Washington Square Press, Inc., New York, 1966.

[7] I have tried to avoid presenting a tiresome catalogue, and only hope that my sins of omission may be absolved by the attempt to maintain a certain unity for the book as a whole.

FOREWORD

WE ARE APT to think of the twentieth century as a time of
esthetic experiments. The word "experiment" is, on the
whole, a wise and a tactful one, since it implies daring and
nearly hints at failure. How else could we refer, without
impertinence, to such major achievements as those of
Pound, Joyce, and Gertrude Stein? Conversely, we are apt
to forget that the nineteenth century was also a century
of experiments. The oversight may easily be explained by
the fact that many of the experiments were successful, and
that when something turns out well one tends to think of
it as obvious, and perhaps inevitable. Poe, by the simple
expedient of supposing that murders could be solved by
pure logic, created the detective novel; Browning's idea
of a story told by the characters and subtly modified in
the telling, revealed the significance of the point of view.
Poets as diverse as Swinburne and Hopkins discovered
a new music. The list is, of course, tentative; the point
I would like to make is that, of all experiments attempted
since James MacPherson composed his *Ossian*, the
strangest is, if we look closely into it, Walt Whitman's
Leaves of Grass.

FOREWORD

Some twenty years before its publication, Emerson, in a famous address, prophesied with uncanny precision the advent of the poet of America. The fact that Whitman became the prophecy should not be used against him; the concrete deed is greater than any definition. In 1855 Whitman, until then an obscure journalist and occasional writer, conceived the project of a vast epic of America and the democracy it stood for. In the second of the many inscriptions of his book, he tells us how the Muse of Epic, "terrible in beauty, age, and power," declares to him that War is the "one theme for ever-enduring bards," and he answers thus:

I too haughty Shade also sing war, and a longer and greater
               one than any,
Waged in my book with varying fortune, with flight, advance
               and retreat, victory deferr'd and wavering,
(Yet methinks certain, or as good as certain, at the last), the
               field the world . . .

and later on we read:

I heard that you ask'd for something to prove this puzzle the
               New World,
And to define America, her athletic Democracy,
Therefore I send you my poems that you behold in them what
               you wanted.

The task at hand was, thus, epic; his solution, not less so. Poetry until then had required a hero, a man looming larger than his fellows: Achilles, Ulysses, Æneas, Beowulf, Roland, the Cid, and Sigurd stand out for our admiration. Clearly this tradition would run counter to the very essence of democracy; the new society demanded a new kind of hero. Whitman's response was an amazing one: he himself would be the hero of the poem—first, as common circumstance had made him, as an American of his time;

second, as magnified by hope, by joy, by exultation, and
by the proud, full sail of his great verse:

Starting from fish-shape Paumanok where I was born,
well-begotten, and rais'd by a perfect mother,
After roaming many lands, lover of populous pavements,
Dweller in Mannahatta my city, or on southern savannas,
Or a soldier camp'd or carrying my knapsack and gun, or a
        miner in California,
Or rude in my home in Dakota's woods, my diet meat, my
        drink from the spring,
Or withdrawn to muse and meditate in some deep recess,
Far from the clank of crowds intervals passing rapt and
        happy,
Aware of the fresh free giver, the flowing Missouri, aware of
        mighty Niagara,
Aware of the buffalo herds grazing the plains, the hirsute and
        strong-breasted bull,
Of earth, rocks, Fifth-month flowers experienced, stars, rain,
        snow, my amaze,
Having studied the mocking-bird's tones and the flight of the
        mountain-hawk,
And heard at dawn the unrivall'd one, the hermit thrush from
        the swamp-cedars,
Solitary, singing in the West, I strike up for a New World.

Here, both strands are interwoven: biography soars into
mythology. Whitman, as we know, was born in Long Is-
land, and loved New York; southern savannas, the miner's
or the soldier's life, and the lonely places of the West were
only real to him through his dreams. In "Song of Myself"
we read:

Now I tell what I knew in Texas in my early youth,
(I tell not the fall of Alamo,
Not one escaped to tell the fall of Alamo,
The hundred and fifty are dumb yet at Alamo,) . . .

Now indeed the verse has taken over: the Whitman of the
book is every American.

FOREWORD

This, however, was not sufficient. A third person was added; Walt Whitman became not only the writer of the book and the splendid shadow projected by him, but also the reader, any reader, any one of his present or future readers. How this was done we shall never quite know. Whitman felt very keenly the strangeness of the link between the man who reads a book and the unknown or dead man who wrote it; this may have helped him to work the miracle he needed. He makes the reader speak to him:

What do you hear, Walt Whitman? . . .

What do you see, Walt Whitman? . . .

and he assures him of his friendship:

I bequeath myself to the dirt to grow from the grass I love,
If you want me again look for me under your boot-soles.

You will hardly know who I am or what I mean,
But I shall be good health to you nevertheless,
and filter and fibre your blood.

Failing to fetch me at first keep encouraged,
Missing me one place search another,
I stop somewhere waiting for you.

Edgar Allan Poe, Whitman's great contemporary, tried to be extraordinary; Whitman, with a gigantic humility that somehow widened into pantheism, tried to be Everyman:

These are really the thoughts of all men in all ages and lands,
    they are not original with me,
If they are not yours as much as mine they are nothing, or
    next to nothing,
If they are not the riddle and the untying of the riddle they
    are nothing,
If they are not just as close as they are distant they are
    nothing.

FOREWORD

This is the grass that grows wherever the land is and the
        water is,
This is the common air that bathes the globe.

This is the meal equally set, this is the meat for natural
        hunger,
It is for the wicked just the same as the righteous, I make
        appointments with all,
I will not have a single person slighted or left away,
The kept-woman, sponger, thief, are hereby invited,
The heavy-lipp'd slave is invited, the venerealee is invited . . .

I have insisted on the threefold nature of the hero of
the book since the writer has integrated his three persons
so perfectly that they can hardly be separated. To our
imagination, Walt Whitman is, indeed, as individual and
complex a creation as Don Quijote, Hamlet, or Peer Gynt.

The enthusiastic reader who passes from the divine
vagabond of *Leaves of Grass* to the Whitman of the *Specimen Days* and the biographers feels, significantly, let
down. It may be a happiness to think that even as the
reading of books of chivalry made a Spanish country
gentleman into Don Quijote, so the writing of *Leaves of
Grass* made the editor of the Brooklyn *Daily Eagle* into
Walt Whitman, into America, into all of us.

Strange to say, Whitman has many imitators—and no
disciples. People think that they are Walt Whitman if
they are sufficiently breezy, slangy, and unmetrical. The
plan of making a character out of the writer and the
reader has not been attempted again; and, for all we
know, it may be impossible.

Jorge Luis Borges

Cambridge, Massachusetts
April 3, 1968

HOMENAJE A WALT WHITMAN / HOMAGE TO
WALT WHITMAN

CAMDEN, 1892

por *Jorge Luis Borges*

El olor del café y de los periódicos.
El domingo y su tedio. La mañana
Y en la entrevista página esa vana
Publicación de versos alegóricos
De una colega feliz. El hombre viejo
Está postrado y blanco en su decente
Habitación de pobre. Ociosamente
Mira su cara en el cansado espejo.
Piensa, ya sin asombro, que esa cara
Es él. La distraída mano toca
La turbia barba y la saqueada boca.
No está lejos el fin. Su voz declara:
Casi no soy, pero mis versos ritman
La vida y su esplendor. Yo fui Walt Whitman.

CAMDEN, 1892

by *Jorge Luis Borges*

The smell of coffee and the daily *Times*.
The Sunday morning tedium, once again,
And on the page, unclearly seen, that vain
Publication of allegoric rhymes
By a happy colleague. On his death-bed,
In his decent though humble bedroom,
The man lies white and wasted. With boredom,
He views the tired reflection of his head.
He thinks, no longer amazed, that this face
Is he, and brings his distrait fingertips
To touch his tarnished beard and ravaged lips.
The end is near, and he states his case:
I hardly am, but my verse is rhythmal
To the splendid life. I was Walt Whitman.

HABLA EL PRÓLOGO

por León Felipe

¿Es inoportuno, amigos y poetas americanos y españoles,
  que yo os congregue aquí ahora y os traiga conmigo al
  viejo comarada de Long Island?
No. Ésta es la hora mejor.
Ahora . . .
cuando avanza el trueno para borrar con trilita la palabra
  libertad, de todos los rincones de la tierra,
cuando el hombre ha perdido su airón y su bandera
y todos somos reses marcadas entre vallados y alambra-
  das,
quiero yo presentaros a este poeta de cabaña
sin puerta frente al camino abierto,
a este poeta de halo, de cayada y de mochila;
ahora . . .
cuando reculan frente al odio el amor y la fe
quiero yo presentaros con verbo castellano, y en mi vieja
  manera de decir,
a este poeta del amor, de la fe y de la rebeldía.
Aquí está. ¡Miradlo!
Se llama Walt.
Así lo nombran
el viento,
los pájaros
y las corrientes de los grandes ríos de su pueblo.
Walt es el diminutivo de Walter (Gualterio en castellano).
Más bien es la poda del patronímico hasta el monosílabo
  simple, onomatopéyico y gutural: Walt.

4

THE PROLOGUE SPEAKS

by León Felipe

Is it inopportune, friends and poets, American or Span-
   ish, that I gather you here today and bring to you
   with me the old comrade from Long Island?
No. This is the best hour.
Now . . .
when the thunder advances to erase with tritium the
   word freedom from all the corners of the earth,
when man has lost his plume and his banner,
and all of us are branded cattle within palings and wire
   fences,
I want to present to you this poet with a cabin
without door facing the open road,
this poet with a halo, with a cane, and a knapsack;
now . . .
when love and faith are yielding to hatred
I want to present to you in my Castilian words, in my old
   manner of speaking,
this poet of love, of faith, and rebellion.
Here he is. Behold him!
His name is Walt.
Thus he is called
by the wind,
the birds,
and the currents of the great rivers of his people.
Walt is the diminutive of Walter (Gualterio in Spanish).
It is rather the pruning of the patronymic to the mono-
   syllable, simple, onomatopoeic and guttural: Walt.

5

CANTARÁ SU CANCIÓN Y SE IRÁ

No tiene otro título ni rótulo a la puerta.
No es doctor,
ni reverendo
ni maese . . .
No es misionero tampoco.
No viene a repartir catecismos ni reglamentos,
ni a colgarle a nadie una cruz en la solapa.
Ni a juzgar:
ni a premiar
ni a castigar.
Viene sencillamente a cantar una canción.

Cantará su canción y se irá.
Mañana, de madrugada, se irá.
Cuando os despertéis vosotros, ya con el sol en el cielo, no
    encontraréis más que el recuerdo encendido de su voz.
Pero esta noche será vuestro huésped.
Abridle la puerta,
los brazos,
los oídos
y el corazón de par en par.
Porque es vuestra canción la que vais a escuchar.

HE SHALL SING HIS SONG AND THEN LEAVE

He has no other title or inscription at his door.
He is not a Doctor,
nor a Reverend,
nor a Master . . .
Neither is he a Missionary.
He does not come to deliver catechisms or laws,
nor to hang a cross on anybody's breast.
Nor to judge
to reward,
or to punish.
He simply comes to sing a song.

He shall sing his song and then leave.
Tomorrow, at dawn, he shall leave.
When you shall awaken, with the sun already up in the
   sky, you shall find nothing but the burning memory
   of his voice.
But tonight he shall be your guest.
Open your door,
your arms,
your ears,
and your heart fully wide.
For the song you shall hear is your song.

FRAGMENTO DE LA INTRODUCCIÓN A
LAS MONTAÑAS DEL ORO

por *Leopoldo Lugones*

El poeta es el astro de su propio destierro.
Él tiene su cabeza junto a Dios, como todos,
Pero su carne es fruto de los cósmicos lodos
De la vida. Su espíritu del mismo yugo es siervo,
Pero en su frente brilla la integridad del Verbo.
Cada vez que una de sus columnas, que en la historia
Trazan nuevos caminos de esfuerzo i de victoria,
Emprende su jornada, dejando detrás de ella
Rastros de lumbre como los pasos de una estrella,
Noches siniestras, ecos de lúgubres clarines,
Huracanes colgados de gigantescas crines
I montes descarnados como imponentes huesos:
Uno de esos engendros del prodigio, uno de esos
Armoniosos doctores del Espíritu Santo,
Alza sobre la cumbre de la noche su canto.
(La alondra i el sol tienen en común estos puntos:
que reinan en los cielos i se levantan juntos.)
El canto de esos grandes es como un tren de guerra
Cuyas sonoras llantas surcan toda la tierra.
Cantan por sus heridas ensangrentadas bocas
De trompetas, que mueven el alma de las rocas
I de los mares. Hugo con su talón fatiga
Los olímpicos potros de su imperial cuadriga;
I, como de un océano que el sol naciente dora,
De sus grandes cabellos se ve surgir la aurora.
Dante alumbra el abismo con su alma. Dante piensa.
Alza entre dos crepúsculos una portada inmensa,

FROM THE INTRODUCTION TO
THE MOUNTAINS OF GOLD

by Leopoldo Lugones

The poet is the star of his own banishment.
He stands close to God, like every fellow man,
but his flesh is fruit of the cosmic morass
of life. His spirit is serf to the same bondage,
but the light of the Word shines on his brow.
Each time one of his columns that march along history,
blazing new trails of effort and victory,
begins on its journey, leaving behind,
traces of fire like the path of a star,
sinister nights, echoes of doleful clarinets,
hurricanes hanging from gigantic manes,
and mountains bare like imposing bones,
one of those monsters of prodigy, one of those
harmonious doctors of the Holy Spirit,
raises his chant above the summits of night.
(The lark and the sun have in common these traits:
they reign in the heavens and they rise together.)
The chant of those great ones is like a train of war
whose sonorous wheels furrow through the whole earth.
Blaring out of their wounds there are bloodied mouths
of trumpets that move the souls of the rocks
and the seas. Hugo drives on with his heel
the Olympic steeds of his imperial chariot,
and as from waters gilded by the rising sun,
from his noble head one sees emerge the dawn.
Dante illumines the abyss with his soul. Dante thinks.
Between twilights, he raises an immense portal,

I pasa, transportando su empresa y sus escombros:
una carga de montes i noches en los hombros.

Whitman entona un canto serenamente noble.
Whitman es el glorioso trabajador del roble.
Él adora la vida que irrumpe en toda siembra,
El grande amor que labra los flancos de la hembra;
I todo cuanto es fuerza, creación, universo,
Pesa sobre las vértebras enormes de su verso.
Homero es la pirámide sonora que sustenta
Los talones de Júpiter, goznes de la tormenta.
Es la boca de lumbre surgiendo del abismo.
Tan de cerca le ha hablado Dios, que él habla lo mismo.

And passes, carrying his work and its remains:
A burden of nights and mountains on his shoulders.

Whitman intones a chant that is serenely noble.
Whitman is the splendid worker of the oak.
He worships the life that springs in every garden,
the great love that labors the flanks of the female,
and all that is power, creation, universe,
rests upon the huge vertebrae of his verse.
Homer is the sonorous pyramid that sustains
the heels of Jupiter, hinges of the storm.
He is the mouth of fire surging up from the deep.
God spoke to him so close, that he speaks as He does.

WALT WHITMAN

por Rubén Darío

En su país de hierro vive el gran viejo,
Bello como un patriarca, sereno y santo.
Tiene en la arruga olímpica de su entrecejo
Algo que impera y vence con noble encanto.

Su alma del infinito parece espejo;
Son sus cansados hombros dignos del manto;
Y con arpa labrada de un roble añejo,
Como un profeta nuevo canta su canto.

Sacerdote que alienta soplo divino,
Anuncia, en el futuro, tiempo mejor.
Dice al águila: "¡Vuela!"; "¡Boga!", al marino,

Y "¡Trabaja!", al robusto trabajador.
¡Así va ese poeta por su camino,
Con su soberbio rostro de emperador!

WALT WHITMAN

by Rubén Darío

In his land of iron lives the great elder,
Beautiful patriarch, serene and holy;
His furrowed brow, of Olympic splendor,
Commands and conquers with noble glory.

His soul, like a mirror, the cosmos evokes,
And his tired shoulders merit the mantle;
With a lyre chiseled from an ancient oak,
As a new prophet he sings his canticles.

A high priest inspired with divine avail
Heralds, in the future, a better spring,
He tells the eagle: "Fly!"; the sailor: "Sail!";

And the robust worker to keep on working.
Thus, the poet passes along his trail,
with the splendid countenance of a king.

WALT WHITMAN

por *Ezequiel Martínez Estrada*

Divagando en los círculos superiores y abstrusos
o bien sencillamente contradictorio y vivo
(todo sabiduría o todo paradoja),
pasas, aunque has "tornado a los eternos usos
de la tierra", esta vez aun más imperativo,
como en la encarnación final de Barbarroja.

Perseguiré tus huellas con la ansiedad del perro
en la tierra que plasma y en los astros que ritman
dondequiera que ahora reproduzcas, Walt Whitman,
las canciones autóctonas de la Isla de Hierro.

Si estás en la bandera constelada y rayada,
o en la reja que vuelca virilmente la gleba,
o en el hito que atisba de pie como un reproche,
o en el nupcial coloquio que aviva la alborada,
o en la tripulación que se arma y se subleva,
o en el tropel de búfalos que atraviesa la noche,
o en el vacío enorme del silencio y la muerte,
recibe este saludo, que hago al azul y al viento
con la impresión segura de abrazarte un momento
y el miedo lacerante de volver a perderte.

WALT WHITMAN

by Ezequiel Martínez Estrada

Wandering among abstruse and upper circles,
or else, simply alive and paradoxical
(all wisdom or all contradiction)
you pass, although you have returned to the "eternal uses
of the earth," this time even more categorical,
as in Barbarossa's final incarnation.

I will follow your trail with the zeal of the hound,
among the rhythmic stars or the earth-molded human,
wherever you are now repeating, Walt Whitman,
the autochthonous canticles of your iron land.

Whether you are in the banner of the stars and stripes,
or at the iron gate where the serfs are rebelling,
or at the post that watches upstanding in defiance,
or at the nuptial exchange which the morning revives,
or with the sailors' crew taking arms and uprising,
or in the trampling of bisons crossing the darkness,
or in the endless void where silence and death reign,
receive this salutation cast to the wind and the sky
with the certain impression of embracing you briefly
and the agonizing fear of losing you again.

LECTURA DE WALT WHITMAN

por Alfredo Cardona Peña

Poderoso y solar, innumerable y uno,
bañando rocas verdes y llanuras, países,
coros nupciales bajo la mañana,
se levanta del mar y millones de seres
el pequeño gigante sorprendido.

Padre andante y pluvial, los cielos ha mojado
con lengua, tambor y callado rocío:
América le debe un ramo de banderas,
una sangre mundial, un vino ciudadano.

Mágico fue, surcado de potentes gaviotas,
fuerte, espectacular, con sabor a desfile
y a circo debutando con focas y luceros.
No obstante celebraba el cumpleaños del río,
la tesis del volcán y el amor de la hierba.
(Fue su verdad un lirio entre motores
y un gran incendio de miradas rojas.)

En su pecho habitaron misteriosos planetas,
perezas de crepúsculo, rosas de inmensidad.
Las razas se paraban a escuchar sus diamantes
y viajaban en él como en un trasatlántico.

La estatua de su poesía está hecha de pueblos,
la vida la esculpió con un mazo de viento:
tiene por ojos las esferas de la noche
y por pies la raíz amorosa del bosque.

A READING OF WALT WHITMAN

by Alfredo Cardona Peña

Powerful and solar, numberless and one,
bathing green rocks and plains and countries,
—nuptial choirs beneath the morning—
surprised, the small giant
arises from the sea and millions of beings.

Pluvial and errant father, he has damped the skies
with tongue, drums, and a silent dew.
America owes him a cluster of banners,
a universal blood, a civil wine.

Magical he was, crossed by mighty seagulls,
strong, spectacular, with a taste of parade,
and of circus debut with seals and stars.
And yet, he celebrated the birthday of the river,
the volcano's thesis and the love of the grass.
(His truth was a lily surrounded by motors
and a great conflagration of red glances.)

His breast was inhabited by mysterious planets,
lassitudes of twilight and roses of immensity.
The races of the Earth stopped to hear his diamonds
and traveled on him as on an ocean liner.

The statue of his poetry is made of peoples.
It was sculptured by life with a hammer of wind:
It has for eyes the spheres of the night,
and for feet, the amorous root of the forest.

Los brazos son dos ríos, la frente un Capitolio,
en la boca amanece la piel de la campana.
Lleva en la mano blanca la cabeza de un niño
y en la roja los arcos de la ciudad futura.

Oh lecho de timbales, oh espléndido monarca
de los cabellos grises,
oh poesía flotando
como una gran ballena tragadora de ancianos.
Tu voz es una piel infinita y despierta,
un avión arrojando propagandas azules:
sale del mar, multiplica en las almas su rostro
y abraza con cien dedos la cintura del mundo.

The arms are two rivers; a capitol its brow;
in its mouth dawns the skin of the bell.
It carries in its white hand the head of a child,
and in the red one the arches of the future city.

Oh bed of cymbals, oh splendid monarch
with graying head.
Oh poetry floating
like a great leviathan, swallower of patriarchs.
Your voice is an endless and awakened skin;
an airplane dropping blue leaflets.
It comes out from the sea, multiplies its face in the
    souls,
and encircles the waist of the world with a hundred
    fingers.

ODA A WALT WHITMAN

por Federico García Lorca

Por el East River y el Bronx
los muchachos cantaban enseñando sus cinturas
con la rueda, el aceite, el cuero y el martillo.
Noventa mil mineros sacaban la plata de las rocas
y los niños dibujaban escaleras y perspectivas.

Pero ninguno se dormía,
ninguno quería ser río,
ninguno amaba las hojas grandes,
ninguno la lengua azul de la playa.

Por el East River y el Queensborough
los muchachos luchaban con la industria,
y los judíos vendían al fauno del río
la rosa de la circuncisión,
y el cielo desembocaba por los puentes y los tejados
manadas de bisontes empujadas por el viento.

Pero ninguno se detenía,
ninguno quería ser nube,
ninguno buscaba los helechos
ni la rueda amarilla del tamboril.

Cuando la luna salga,
las poleas rodarán para turbar el cielo;
un límite de agujas cercará la memoria
y los ataúdes se llevarán a los que no trabajan.

Nueva York de cieno,
Nueva York de alambre y de muerte:

ODE TO WALT WHITMAN

by Federico García Lorca

Along East River and the Bronx
the youths were singing, showing their waists,
with the leather, the hammer, the wheel and the oil.
Ninety thousand miners mined silver from the rocks,
and the children were drawing ladders and perspectives.

But no one would sleep,
no one wished to be a river,
no one loved the big leaves,
nor the beach's blue tongue.

Along East River and Queensborough,
the youths were struggling with Industry,
the Jews were selling to the faun of the river
the rose of circumcision,
and the skies emptied over bridges and rooftops
herds of bison driven by the wind.

But no one would pause,
no one wished to be a cloud,
no one looked for the ferns
nor the yellow wheel of the tambourine.

When the moon has risen,
the pulleys will turn to disturb the sky,
a boundary of needles will confine the memory,
and coffins will remove those who do not work.

Slimy New York,
New York of wires and death.

¿qué angel llevas oculto en la mejilla?
¿qué voz perfecta dirá las verdades del trigo?
¿quién, el sueño terrible de tus anémonas manchadas?

Ni un sólo momento, viejo hermoso Walt Whitman
he dejado de ver tu barba llena de mariposas,
ni tus hombros de pana gastados por la luna,
ni tus muslos de Apolo virginal,
ni tu voz como una columna de ceniza;
anciano hermoso como la niebla,
que gemías igual que un pájaro
con el sexo atravesado por una aguja.
Enemigo del sátiro.
Enemigo de la vid,
y amante de los cuerpos bajo la burda tela.

Ni un sólo momento; hermosura viril
que en montes de carbón, anuncios y ferrocarriles,
soñabas con ser río y dormir como un río
con aquel camarada que pondría en tu pecho
un pequeño dolor de ignorante leopardo.

Ni un sólo momento, Adán de sangre, macho,
hombre solo en el mar, viejo hermoso Walt Whitman,
porque por las azoteas,
agrupados en los bares,
saliendo en racimos de las alcantarillas,
temblando entre las piernas de los chauffeurs
o girando en las plataformas de ajenjo,
los maricas, Walt Whitman, te señalan.

¡También ése! ¡También! Y se despeñan
sobre tu barba luminosa y casta,
rubios del norte, negros de la arena,
muchedumbre de gritos y ademanes
como los gatos y como las serpientes
los maricas, Walt Whitman, los maricas,

What angel do you carry concealed in your cheek?
What perfect voice will speak the truths of the wheat?
Who, the terrible dream of your stained anemones?

Not a single moment, handsome elder Walt Whitman,
have I ceased to envision your beard, full of butterflies,
your corduroy shoulders, frayed thin by the moon,
your virginal, Appollonian thighs,
your voice, like a pillar of ashes;
patriarch, handsome as the fog,
who cried like a bird
whose sex had been pierced by a needle.
Satyr's enemy,
grapevine's enemy,
and lover of bodies under the coarse cloth.

Not a single moment, masculine beauty,
who on mountains of coal, billboards and railroads,
dreamed of being a river, and sleeping like a river,
alongside that comrade who would set in your heart
the faint aching of an ignorant leopard.

Not a single moment, blood-Adam, he-man,
lone man in the sea, handsome elder Walt Whitman,
for on the rooftops,
or huddled in bars,
or coming out in clusters from the gutters,
or trembling between chauffeurs' legs,
or whirling on platforms of absinthe,
the *fairies*, Walt Whitman, are pointing at you.

That one also! That one! And they fall
upon your chaste and luminous beard,
blonds from the North, blacks from the sand,
crowd of gestures and shrieks,
like cats and snakes,
—the *fairies*, Walt Whitman, the *fairies*—

23

turbios de lágrimas, carne para fusta,
bota o mordisco de los domadores.

¡También ése! ¡También! Dedos teñidos
apuntan a la orilla de tu sueño
cuando el amigo come tu manzana
con un leve sabor de gasolina,
y el sol canta por los ombligos
de los muchachos que juegan bajo los puentes.
Pero tú no buscabas los ojos arañados,
ni el pantano oscurísimo donde sumergen a los niños,
ni la saliva helada,
ni las curvas heridas como panza de sapo
que llevan los maricas en coches y en terrazas,
mientras la luna los azota por las esquinas del terror.

Tú buscabas un desnudo que fuera como un río,
toro y sueño que junte la rueda con el alga,
padre de tu agonía, camelia de tu muerte
y gimiera en las llamas de tu ecuador oculto.

Porque es justo que el hombre no busque su deleite
en las selvas de sangre de la mañana próxima.
El cielo tiene playas donde evitar la vida,
y hay cuerpos que no deben repetirse en la aurora.

Agonía, agonía, sueño, fermento y sueño.
Este es el mundo, amigo, agonía, agonía.
Los muertos se descomponen bajo el reloj de las
    ciudades.
La guerra pasa llorando con un millón de ratas grises,
los ricos dan a sus queridas
pequeños moribundos iluminados,
y la vida no es noble, ni buena, ni sagrada.
Puede el hombre, si quiere, conducir su deseo
por vena de coral o celeste desnudo;
mañana los amores serán rocas y el tiempo
una brisa que viene dormida por las ramas.

grimy with tears, flesh for the whiplash,
the boot or the bite of the animal-tamers.

That one also! That one! Stained fingers
point to the edge of your dream
when the friend eats your apple
with a faint taste of gasoline
and the sunlight sings upon the navels
of youths playing under bridges.
But you were not looking for the scratched eyes,
nor the darksome swamp where the boys are immersed,
nor the icy saliva,
nor the broken curves, like a toad's belly,
paraded by *fairies* in taxis and terraces
while the moon lashes at them round the corners of terror.

You looked for a nude that would be like a river,
bull and dream to join the sea-weed and the wheel,
sire of your agony, camellia of your death,
and would moan in the flames of your hidden Equator.

It is fitting that man should not seek his pleasure
in the bloody jungles of the morning after.
The sky has beaches to escape from life,
and there are bodies which must not be repeated at dawn.

Agony, agony, dream, ferment and dream.
This is the world, my friend: agony, agony.
Dead bodies decay under the clock of the cities.
War passes weeping with a million gray rats.
Rich men give their mistresses
small illuminated moribunds,
and life is not noble, nor wholesome, nor holy.

Man could, if he wished, convey his desire
through vein of coral or celestial nude.
Tomorrow, our loves will be rocks, and Time,
a breeze which comes sleeping through the branches.

25

Por eso no levanto mi voz, viejo Walt Whitman,
contra el niño que escribe
nombre de niña en su almohada;
ni contra el muchacho que se viste de novia
en la oscuridad del ropero;
ni contra los solitarios de los casinos
que beben con asco el agua de la prostitución;
ni contra los hombres de mirada verde
que aman al hombre y queman sus labios en silencio.
Pero sí contra vosotros, maricas de las ciudades,
de carne tumefacta y pensamiento inmundo.
Madres de lodo. Arpías. Enemigos sin sueño
del Amor que reparte coronas de alegrías.

Contra vosotros siempre, que dais a los muchachos
gotas de sucia muerte con amargo veneno.
Contra vosotros siempre,
"fairies" de Norteamérica,
"pájaros" de La Habana,
"jotos" de Méjico,
"sarasas" de Cádiz,
"apios" de Sevilla,
"cancos" de Madrid,
"floras" de Alicante,
"adelaidas" de Portugal.

¡Maricas de todo el mundo, asesinos de palomas!
Esclavos de la mujer. Perras de sus tocadores.
abiertos en las plazas, con fiebre de abanico,
o emboscados en yertos paisajes de cicuta.

¡No haya cuartel! La muerte
mana de vuestros ojos
y agrupa flores grises en la orilla del cieno.
¡No haya cuartel! ¡Alerta!
Que los confundidos, los puros,
los clásicos, los señalados, los suplicantes
os cierren las puertas de la bacanal.

26

Therefore, I do not raise my voice, elder Walt Whitman,
against the boy who inscribes
a girl's name on his pillow,
nor against the youth dressing like a bride
in the dark of the closet,
nor against the lonely ones in the men's club
who drink with repugnance at the waters of whoredom,
nor against the men with a look of lust
who love man and burn their lips in silence.
But certainly against you, *fairies* of the cities,
tumescent of flesh and foul of thought.
Mothers of filth. Harpies. Sleepless enemies
of Love who bestows upon us garlands of happiness.

Always against you, who give to the boys
drops of foul death with bitter venom.
Against you; always!
Fairies of North America,
pájaros of Havana,
jotos of Mexico,
sarasas of Cádiz
apios of Seville,
cancos of Madrid,
floras of Alicante,
adelaidas of Portugal.

Fairies of the world, dove-killers!
Toadies of women, dressing-room bitches,
displayed in public squares with a fever of fans,
or ambushed in still landscapes of hemlock.

No quarter! Death
oozes out of your eyes
and clusters gray flowers at the edge of the mire.
No quarter! Beware!
Let the pure, the bewildered,
the classic, the selected, the suppliant
close to you the gates of the Bacchanalia.

Y tú, bello Walt Whitman, duerme a orillas del Hudson,
con la barba hacia el polo y las manos abiertas.
Arcilla blanda o nieve tu lengua está llamando
camaradas que velen tu gacela sin cuerpo.

Duerme: No queda nada.
Una danza de muros agita las praderas
y América se anega de máquinas y llanto.
Quiero que el aire fuerte de la noche más honda
quite flores y letras del arco donde duermes,
y un niño negro anuncie a los blancos del oro
la llegada del reino de la espiga.

And you, beautiful Walt Whitman, sleep yet on the
    Hudson's shore,
with your beard to the Pole, and your hands open.
Soft clay or snow, your tongue is summoning
comrades to keep vigil for your incorporeal gazelle.

Sleep on. Nothing remains.
A dancing of walls stirs the meadows
and America drowns in machines and tears.
I call for the strong wind from the deepest of nights
to clear away flowers and letters from the arch where
    you sleep
and a black child to announce to the golden whites
the coming of the kingdom of the wheat.

SELECCIONES DE
CONTRACANTO A WALT WHITMAN:
CANTO A NOSOTROS MISMOS
por Pedro Mir

1

HUBO UNA VEZ UN TERRITORIO PURO.
Árboles y terrones sin rúbricas ni alambres.
Hubo una vez un territorio sin tacha.
Hace ya muchos años. Más allá de los padres de los
    padres.
Las llanuras jugaban a galopes de búfalos.
Las costas infinitas jugaban a las perlas.
Las rocas desceñían su vientre de diamantes.
Y las lomas jugaban a cabras y gacelas . . .

Por los claros del bosque la brisa regresaba
cargada de insolencias de ciervos y abedules
que henchían de simiente los poros de la tarde,
Y era una tierra pura poblada de sorpresas.
Donde un terrón tocaba la semilla
precipitaba un bosque de dulzura fragante.
Le acometía a veces un frenesí de polen
que exprimía los álamos, los pinos, los abetos,
y enfrascaba en racimos la noche y los paisajes.
Y eran minas y bosques y praderas
cundidos de arroyuelos y nubes y animales.

6

¡OH, WALT WHITMAN, tu barba sensitiva
era una red al viento!
Vibraba y se llenaba de encendidas figuras
de novias y donceles, de bravos y labriegos,
de rudos mozalbetes camino del riachuelo,

SELECTIONS FROM
COUNTERSONG TO WALT WHITMAN:
SONG OF OURSELVES
by *Pedro Mir*

1

ONCE UPON A TIME THERE WAS A PURE LAND.
Trees and soil with neither names nor fences.
Once upon a time there was a faultless land.
Many years ago. Long before the fathers of the fathers.
The prairies played a game of galloping buffaloes.
The endless shorelines played a game of pearls.
The rocks unfastened their diamond wombs.
And the hills played a game of goats and gazelles . . .

Through the clearings in the forest, the breeze returned
charged with the insolence of deers and birch-trees
filling with seeds the pores of the evening.
And it was a pure land, peopled with surprises.
Where a clod of earth touched the seed,
it precipitated a sweet fragrant forest.
At times it was seized with a frenzy of pollen
that squeezed the poplars, the pines, the silver-trees,
and entangled in clusters nights and landscapes.
And there were mines and forests and meadows
abundantly filled with rivulets and clouds and animals.

6

OH WALT WHITMAN, your sensitive beard
was a net in the wind!
It quivered and filled with flaming figures
of brides and sweet youths, of brave men and farmers,
of rustic lads walking to the streams,

31

de guapos con espuelas y mozas con sonrisa,
de marchas presurosas de seres infinitos,
de trenzas o sombreros . . .
Y tú fuiste escuchando
camino por camino
golpeándoles el pecho
palabra con palabra.
¡Oh, Walt Whitman de barba candorosa,
alcanzo por los años tu roja llamarada!

9

PORQUE
    ¿qué ha sido un gran poeta indeclinable
      si no un estanque límpido
        donde un pueblo descubre su perfecto
        semblante
¿qué ha sido
        si no un parque sumergido
          donde todos los hombres se reconocen
              por el lenguaje?
¿y qué
    si no una cuerda de infinita guitarra
      donde pulsan los dedos de los pueblos
        su sencilla, su propia, su fuerte y
          verdadera canción innumerable?
Por eso tú, numeroso Walt Whitman, que viste y deliraste
la palabra precisa para cantar tu pueblo,
que en medio de la noche dijiste

yo

y el pescador se comprendió en su capa
y el cazador se oyó en mitad de su disparo
y el leñador se conoció en su hacha
y el labriego en su siembra y el lavador
de oro en su semblante amarillo sobre el agua

of he-men with spurs and maidens with smiles,
of impetuous marches of infinite beings,
of tresses or hats . . .
And you went listening
road after road,
striking their chests,
word after word.
Oh Walt Whitman with candid beard,
I reach through the years your red blaze of fire!

9

FOR
>   what else is a great, inevitable poet
>   but a limpid pool
>   where a people discover their perfect image?
What else
>   but a submerged garden
>   where all men recognize themselves
>   in language?
And what else
>   but a chord of an endless guitar
>   where the people's fingers pluck
>   their simple, their own, their
>   strong and
>   their true, innumerable song?
For that reason, you, numerous Walt Whitman, who
    saw and dreamed
the precise word for singing your people,
who in the midst of night said

I

and the fisherman understood himself in his cape
and the hunter heard himself in the midst of his shot
and the wood-cutter recognized himself in his axe
and the farmer in his field and the gold-
panner in his yellow image on the water

y la doncella en su ciudad futura

que crece y que madura

bajo la saya
y la meretriz en su fuente de alegría
y el minero de sombra en sus pasos debajo de la
    patria . . .
cuando el alto predicador, bajando la cabeza,
entre dos largas manos, decía

yo

y se encontraba unido al fundidor y al vendedor
y al caminante oscuro de suave polvareda
y al soñador y al trepador
y al albañil terrestre parecido a una lápida
y al labrador y al tejedor
y al marinero blanco parecido a un pañuelo . . .
Y el pueblo entero se miraba a sí mismo
cuando escuchaba la palabra

yo

y el pueblo entero se escuchaba en ti mismo
cuando escuchaba la palabra

yo, Walt Whitman, un cosmos,
un hijo de Manhattan.

Porque tú eras el pueblo, tú eras yo,
y yo era la Democracia, el apellido del pueblo,
y yo era también Walt Whitman, un cosmos,
un hijo de Manhattan . . . !

15

Y AHORA
ya no es la palabra

34

and the maiden in her future city
                              that grows and matures
underneath her skirt
and the prostitute in her fountain of joy
and the miner of shadows in his steps below the
                                        Fatherland . . .
When the tall preacher, bowing his head,
between two long hands, said

I

and found himself united to the metal forger and to the
    salesman,
to the obscure wanderer in a soft cloud of dust,
to the dreamer and the climber,
to the earthy bricklayer who resembles a gravestone,
to the farmer and the weaver,
to the sailor in white who resembles a handkerchief . . .
And all the people saw themselves
when they heard the word

I

and all the people listened to themselves in your song
when they listened to the word
                        I, Walt Whitman, a cosmos
                        of Manhattan the son.
Because you were the people, you were I,
and I was Democracy, the people's last name,
and I was also Walt Whitman, a cosmos
of Manhattan the son . . . !

15

AND NOW
it is no longer the word

                    yo

la palabra cumplida
la palabra de toque para empezar el mundo.
Y ahora
ahora es la palabra
                    n o s o t r o s.
Y ahora,
ahora es llegada la hora del c o n t r a c a n t o.

        Nosotros los ferroviarios,
        nosotros los estudiantes,
        nosotros los mineros,
        nosotros los campesinos,
        nosotros los pobres de la tierra,
        los pobladores del mundo,
        los héroes del trabajo cotidiano,
        con nuestro amor y con nuestros puños,
        enamorados de la esperanza.
        Nosotros los blancos,
        los negros, los amarillos,
        los indios, los cobrizos,
        los moros y morenos,
        los rojos y aceitunados,
        los rubios y los platinos,
        unificados por el trabajo,
        por la miseria, por el silencio,
        por el grito de un hombre solitario
        que en medio de la noche,
        con un perfecto látigo,
        con un salario oscuro,
        con un puñal de oro y un semblante de hierro,
        desenfrenadamente grita

                            yo

        y siente el eco cristalino
        de una ducha de sangre

the accomplished word,
the touch-word to begin the world.
And now,
now it is the word
                    w e .
And now,
now has come the hour of the c o u n t e r s o n g .

    We, the railroad workers,
    we, the students,
    we, the miners,
    we, the peasants,
    we, the poor of the earth,
    populators of the world,
    daily-work heroes,
    with our love and our fists,
    enamoured of hope.
    We, the whites,
    the blacks, the yellow,
    the Indians, the bronze,
    Moorish and brunette,
    olive and red,
    platinum and blond,
    united by work,
    by misery, by silence,
    by the shout of a solitary man
    who in the midst of night
    with a perfect whip,
    with a dark salary,
    with a golden knife and an iron face,
    unrestrainedly shouts

                    I

    and feels the crystalline echo
    of a shower of blood

que decididamente se alimenta en

                                    nosotros
y en medio de los muelles alejándose

                                    nosotros
y al pie del horizonte de las fábricas

                                    nosotros
y en la flor y en los cuadros y en los túneles

                                    nosotros
y en la alta estructura camino de las órbitas

                                    nosotros
camino de los mármoles

                                    nosotros
camino de las cárceles

                                    nosotros

17

¿POR QUÉ queríais escuchar a un poeta?
Estoy hablando con unos y con otros.
Con aquellos que vinieron a apartarlo de su pueblo,
a separarlo de su sangre y de su tierra,
a inundarle su camino.
Aquellos que lo inscribieron en el ejército.
Los que violaron su barba luminosa y le pusieron un fusil
sobre sus hombros cargados de doncellas y pioneros.
Los que no quieren a Walt Whitman el demócrata,
sino a un tal Whitman atómico y salvaje.
Los que quieren ponerle zapatones
para aplastar la cabeza de los pueblos.
Moler en sangre las sienes de las niñas.
Desintegrar en átomos las fibras del abuelo.
Los que toman la lengua de Walt Whitman
por signo de metralla,
por bandera de fuego.

               which decidedly feeds on
                                    us
in the midst of wharfs that reach far away
                                    us
and below the horizon of the factories
                                    us
in the flower, in the pictures, in the tunnels
                                    us
in the tall structure on the way to the orbits
                                    us
on the way to the marbles
                                    us
on the way to the prisons
                                    us

17

WHY did you want to listen to a poet?
I speak with these and with the others.
With those who came to take him away from his people,
to separate him from his blood and his land,
to inundate his way.
Those who registered him in the army.
Those who defiled his luminous beard and put a rifle
on his shoulders that were laden with maids and
    pioneers.
Those who do not want the democratic Walt Whitman
but an atomic and savage Whitman.
Those who want to fit him big shoes
to crush the heads of the peoples,
to pound in blood the temples of the little girls,
to break in atoms the grandfather's fibers.
Those who take the tongue of Walt Whitman
as a sign of shooting,
as a flag of fire.

¡No, Walt Whitman, aquí están los poetas de hoy
levantados para justificarte!
"—¡Poetas venideros, levantaos, porque vosotros debéis
justificarme!"
Aquí estamos, Walt Whitman, para justificarte.
Aquí estamos

          por ti

             pidiendo paz.
La paz que requerías
para empujar el mundo con tu canto.
Aquí estamos

            salvando tus colinas de Vermont,
tus selvas de Maine, el zumo y la fragancia de tu tierra,
tus guapos con espuelas, tus mozas con sonrisa,
tus rudos mozalbetes camino del riachuelo.
Salvándolos, Walt Whitman, de los traficantes
que toman tu lenguaje por lenguaje de guerra.
¡No, Walt Whitman, aquí están los poetas de hoy,
los obreros de hoy, los pioneros de hoy, los campesinos
de hoy,

            firmes y levantados para justificarte!
¡Oh, Walt Whitman de barba levantada!
Aquí estamos sin barba,
sin brazos, sin oído,
sin fuerzas en los labios,
mirados de reojo,
rojos y perseguidos,
llenos de pupilas
que a través de las islas se dilatan,
llenos de coraje, de nudos de soberbia
que a través de los pueblos se desatan,
con tu signo y tu idioma de Walt Whitman
aquí estamos
en pie
para justificarte,
continuo compañero de Manhattan!

40

No, Walt Whitman, here are the poets of today
aroused to justify you!
"—Poets to come! . . . Arouse! for you must
justify me!"
Here we are, Walt Whitman, to justify you.
Here we are
                    in your place
                              asking for peace.
The peace that you required
to push the world with your song.
Here we are
                    saving your hills of Vermont,
your woods of Maine, the juice and fragrance of your
    land,
your he-men with spurs, your maidens with smiles,
your rustic lads walking to the streams.
Saving them, Walt Whitman, from the merchants
who take your language as a language of war.
No, Walt Whitman, here are the poets of today,
workers of today, pioneers of today, peasants
of today,
                    firm and aroused to justify you!
Oh Walt Whitman with aroused beard!
Here we are without beards,
without arms, without ears,
without strength in our lips,
suspiciously watched,
red and persecuted,
full of pupils
dilated throughout the islands,
full of courage, of knots of pride
untied throughout the nations,
with your sign and your language, Walt Whitman
here we are,
standing up
to justify you,
constant companion from Manhattan!

41

ODA A WALT WHITMAN

por Pablo Neruda

Yo no recuerdo
a qué edad,
ni dónde,
si en el gran Sur mojado
o en la costa
temible, bajo el breve
grito de las gaviotas,
toqué una mano y era
la mano de Walt Whitman:
pisé la tierra
con los pies desnudos,
anduve sobre el pasto,
sobre el firme rocío
de Walt Whitman.

Durante
mi juventud
toda
me acompañó esa mano,
ese rocío,
su firmeza de pino patriarca, su extensión de pradera,
y su misión de paz circulatoria.

Sin
desdeñar
los dones
de la tierra,
la copiosa
curva del capitel,

ODE TO WALT WHITMAN

by Pablo Neruda

I do not remember
at what age
nor where:
in the great damp South
or on the fearsome
coast, beneath the brief
cry of the seagulls,
I touched a hand and it was
the hand of Walt Whitman.
I trod the ground
with bare feet,
I walked on the grass,
on the firm dew
of Walt Whitman.

During
my entire
youth
I had the company of that hand,
that dew,
its firmness of patriarchal pine, its prairie-like expanse,
and its mission of circulatory peace.

Not
disdaining
the gifts
of the earth,
nor the copious
curving of the column's capital,

43

ni la inicial
purpúrea
de la sabiduría,
tú
me enseñaste
a ser americano,
levantaste
mis ojos
a los libros,
hacia
el tesoro
de los cereales:
ancho,
en la claridad
de las llanuras,
me hiciste ver
el alto
monte
tutelar. Del eco
subterráneo,
para mí
recogiste
todo,
todo lo que nacía
cosechaste
galopando en la alfalfa,
cortando para mí las amapolas,
visitando
los ríos,
acudiendo en la tarde
a las cocinas.

Pero no sólo
tierra
sacó a la luz
tu pala:

44

nor the purple
initial
of wisdom,
you taught me
to be an American,
you raised
my eyes
to books,
towards
the treasure
of the grains:
broad,
in the clarity
of the plains,
you made me see
the high
tutelary
mountain. From subterranean
echoes,
you gathered
for me
everything;
everything that came forth
was harvested by you,
galloping in the alfalfa,
picking poppies for me,
visiting
the rivers,
coming into the kitchens
in the afternoon.

But not only
soil
was brought to light
by your spade:

desenterraste
al hombre,
y el
esclavo
humillado
contigo, balanceando
la negra dignidad de su estatura,
caminó conquistando
la alegría.

Al fogonero,
abajo,
en la caldera,
mandaste
un canastito
de frutillas,
a todas las esquinas de tu pueblo
un verso
tuyo llegó de visita
y era como un trozo
de cuerpo limpio
el verso que llegaba,
como
tu propia barba pescadora
o el solemne camino de tus piernas de acacia.

Pasó entre los soldados
tu silueta
de bardo, de enfermero,
de cuidador nocturno
que conoce
el sonido
de la respiración en la agonía
y espera con la aurora
el silencioso
regreso
de la vida.

you unearthed
man,
and the
slave
who was humiliated
with you, balancing
the black dignity of his stature,
walked on, conquering
happiness.

To the fireman
below,
in the stoke-hole,
you sent
a little basket
of strawberries.
To every corner of your town
a verse
of yours arrived for a visit,
and it was like a piece
of clean body,
the verse that arrived,
like
your own fisherman beard
or the solemn tread of your acacia legs.

Your silhouette
passed among the soldiers:
the poet, the wound-dresser,
the night attendant
who knows
the sound
of breathing in mortal agony
and awaits with the dawn
the silent
return
of life.

Buen panadero!
Primo hermano mayor
de mis raíces,
cúpula
de araucaria,
hace
ya
cien
años
que sobre el pasto tuyo
y sus germinaciones,
el viento
pasa
sin gastar tus ojos.

Nuevos
y crueles años en tu patria:
persecusiones,
lágrimas,
prisiones,
armas envenenadas
y guerras iracundas,
no han aplastado
la hierba de tu libro,
el manantial vital
de su frescura.
Y, ay!
los
que asesinaron
a Lincoln
ahora
se acuestan en su cama,
derribaron
su sitial
de olorosa madera
y erigieron un trono

Good baker!
Elder first cousin
of my roots,
araucaria's
cupola,
it is
now
a hundred
years
that over your grass
and its germinations,
the wind
passes
without wearing out your eyes

New
and cruel years in your Fatherland:
persecutions,
tears,
prisons,
poisoned weapons
and wrathful wars
have not crushed
the grass of your book;
the vital fountainhead
of its freshness.
And, alas!
those
who murdered
Lincoln
now
lie in his bed.
They felled
his seat of honor
made of fragrant wood,
and raised a throne

por desventura y sangre
salpicado.

Pero
canta en
las estaciones
suburbanas
tu voz,
en
los
desembarcaderos
vespertinos
chapotea
como
agua oscura
tu palabra,
tu pueblo
blanco
y negro,
pueblo
de pobres,
pueblo simple
como
todos
los pueblos,
no olvida
tu campana:
se congrega cantando
bajo
la magnitud
de tu espaciosa vida:
entre los pueblos con tu amor camina
acariciando
el desarrollo puro
de la fraternidad sobre la tierra.

spattered
with misfortune and blood.

But
your voice
sings
in the suburban
stations,
in
the
vespertine
wharfs,
your word
splashes
like
dark water.
Your people,
white
and black,
poor
people,
simple people
like
all
people
do not forget
your bell:
They congregate singing
beneath
the magnitude
of your spacious life.
They walk among the peoples with your love
caressing
the pure development
of brotherhood on earth.

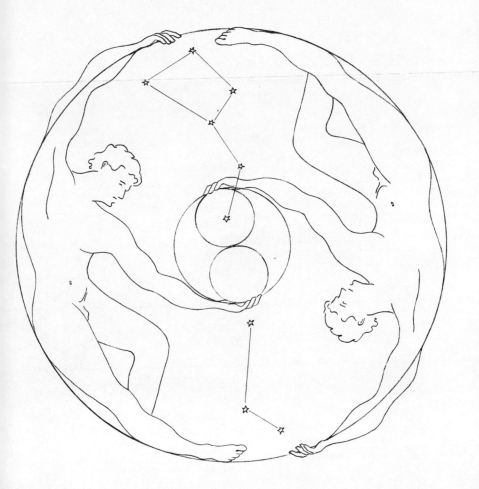

APPENDIX I

"THE POET
WALT WHITMAN"
[*New York,
April 19, 1887*]

by José Martí

"HE LOOKED LIKE A GOD last night, sitting in his red velvet chair, his hair all white, his beard upon his breast, his brows like a thicket, his hand upon a cane." This is what a newspaper says today of the poet Walt Whitman, a man of seventy whom the deeper critics, who are always in the minority, assign to an extraordinary place in the literature of his country and times. Only the holy books of antiquity, with their prophetic language and robust poetry, afford a doctrine comparable to that which is given out in grand, sacerdotal apothegms, like bursts of light, by this elderly poet, whose astounding book has been banned.

And why not, since it is a natural book? Universities and erudition have brought men to such a state that they no longer recognize each other. Instead of throwing themselves into each other's arms, attracted by the essential and eternal, they draw apart, exchanging the flatteries of fishwives, on account of merely accidental differences. Like a pudding in a mold, a man takes on the shape of the energetic teacher or book with which he was brought into contact by chance or by the fashion of his times.

55

Philosophical, religious, or literary schools dress men in their habits, like livery does the footman. Men allow themselves to be branded like horses or bulls, and go around in the world flaunting their mark. Thus, when they find themselves in the presence of a naked, virginal, loving, sincere, and potent man—a man who walks, loves, fights, rows his boat—a man who, not letting himself be blinded by misfortune, reads a promise of final happiness in the balance and harmony of the world; when they find themselves in the presence of Walt Whitman's Father-man, sinewy and angelic, they flee as from their own consciences and refuse to recognize in that fragrant and superior humanity the true type of their own pale, wrapped up, and puppetlike species.

The newspaper says that yesterday, when that other venerable elder, Gladstone, had finished lecturing his rivals in Parliament concerning the rightfulness of granting self-government to Ireland, he looked like a mighty mastiff, standing erect and unchallenged in the midst of the mob, while they lay at his feet like a pack of bull terriers. So seems Whitman, with his "natural persons," with his "Nature without check with original energy," with his "myriads of youths, beautiful, gigantic," with his belief that "the smallest sprout shows there is really no death," with the impressive naming of peoples and races in his "Salut au Monde!," with his resolve that "Knowing the perfect fitness and equanimity of things, while they discuss I am silent, and go bathe and admire myself." So seems Whitman, who does "not say these things for a dollar"; who says, "I am satisfied—I see, dance, laugh, sing"; who has no professorship or pulpit or school. So seems he when compared to the spiritless poets and philosophers, philosophers of the detail or of the single aspect; bookish, standardized, sweetness-and-light poets, philosophical or literary figurines.

APPENDIX I

He should be studied, for while he is not a poet of the most refined taste, he is the most daring, inclusive, and uninhibited of his times. In his frame cottage which stands on the verge of poverty, he displays in a window a portrait of Victor Hugo, bordered in black. Emerson, whose words purify and uplift, used to put his arm on Whitman's shoulder and call him his friend. Tennyson, the kind of man who sees to the roots of things, sends affectionate messages to "the grand old man," from his oaken armchair in England. Robert Buchanan, the Englishman of the fiery words, cries out to the North Americans, "What can you know of literature when you let the old age of your colossal Walt Whitman run out without the honors it deserves?"

The truth is that reading him, although it causes amazement at first, leaves a delightful feeling of convalescence in the soul, which has been tormented by universal pettiness. He creates his own grammar and logic. He reads in the ox's eye and in the sap of a leaf. "The cleaner of privies —that man is my brother!" His apparent irregularity, disconcerting at first, becomes later, except for brief moments of extraordinary frenzy, the sublime order and composition with which mountain peaks loom against the horizon.

He does not live in New York, his "beloved Manhattan," his "superb-faced" and "million-footed" Manhattan, where he looks in whenever he wishes to sing the "song of what I behold Libertad." Cared for by "loving friends," since his books and lectures provide scarcely enough for his daily bread, he lives in a small house nestled in a pleasant country nook. From here, in his carriage drawn by the horses he loves, he goes out to see the "stout young men" at their virile diversions, the "comrades" who are not afraid to rub elbows with this iconoclast who wants to establish "the institution of the dear love of comrades";

to view the fields they till, and the friends who pass by
arm-in-arm, singing; and the sweethearts in couples,
cheerful and lively as partridges. He tells of this in his
"Calamus," that very strange book in which he sings
of the love of friends: "Not the pageants of you, not your
shifting tableaus . . . repay me . . . Nor the processions in
the streets, nor the bright windows with goods in them,
Nor to converse with learn'd persons . . . ; Not those, but
as I pass O Manhattan, your frequent and swift flash of
eyes offering me love, . . . Lovers, continual lovers, only
repay me." He is like the old men whom he announces at
the end of his censored book, his *Leaves of Grass*: "I an-
nounce myriads of youth, beautiful, gigantic, sweet-
blooded; I announce a race of wild and splendid old men."

He lives in the country, where natural man, in the sun-
shine that tans his skin, plows the free earth with his tran-
quil horses; but not far from the friendly, teeming city,
with its life noises, its multiple occupations, its thousand-
fold epic, the dust of its vehicles, the smoke from the pant-
ing factories, the sun looking down on it all, the workers
who talk at lunch on piles of bricks, the ambulance speed-
ing along with the hero who has just fallen from a scaffold,
the woman surprised in the midst of a crowd by the au-
gust pain of maternity.

But yesterday Whitman came from the country to read,
before a gathering of loyal friends, his oration on that
other natural man, that great and gentle soul, that "power-
ful western fallen star!", Abraham Lincoln. All the intel-
lectual elite of New York attended in religious silence that
luminous speech, which for its sudden trills, vibrant
tones, hymnlike fugues, and Olympian familiarity seemed
at times the whispering of stars. Those brought up in the
Latin tradition, whether academic or French, could not
perhaps understand that heroic charm. The free and de-

corous life of man on a new continent has created a whole-
some, robust philosophy that is issuing forth upon the
world in athletic epodes. To the largest number of free,
industrious men that Earth ever witnessed, corresponds a
poetry of inclusiveness and faith, calming and solemn; a
poetry that rises, like the sun out of the sea, kindling the
clouds, rimming the wave crests with fire, awaking the
tired flowers and the nests in the prolific forests of the
shore. Pollen takes wing, beaks exchange kisses; branches
pair together; leaves seek the sun; all creation breathes
music: with such language of rude light Whitman spoke
of Lincoln.

Perhaps one of the most beautiful products of contem-
porary poetry is the mystic threnody Whitman composed
on the death of Lincoln. All Nature accompanies the sor-
rowful coffin on its road to the grave. The stars predicted
it. The clouds had been darkening for a month. In the
swamp a grey-brown bird was singing a song of desola-
tion. Between the thought and the certainty of death the
poet goes through the grieving fields as between two com-
panions. With a musician's art he groups, conceals, and
reproduces these sad elements in a total twilight harmony.
It seems, when the poem is done, as if the whole land has
been clothed in black and the dead man has covered it
from sea to sea. We see the clouds, the heavy moon an-
nouncing the catastrophe, the long wings of the grey-
brown bird. It is much more beautiful, strange, and pro-
found than Poe's "Raven." The poet carries a sprig of
lilacs to the coffin.

Willows no longer weep over graves; death is the har-
vest, the opener, the great revealer. What is now in exist-
ence existed before and will exist again; oppositions and
apparent griefs are blended in a solemn, celestial Spring-
time; a bone is a flower. Close at hand we hear the sound

of suns which with majestic movement seek their definitive station in space; life is a hymn; death is a hidden form of life; the sweat of the brow is holy, and the entozoan is holy; men should kiss one another's cheeks in passing; the living should embrace with ineffable love; they should love the grass, animals, air, sea, pain, death; suffering is less intense for souls possessed by love; life has no sorrows for him who understands its meaning soon enough; honey, light, and a kiss are of the same seed. In the darkness that sparkles peacefully like a vault studded with stars, to soft music, over worlds asleep like hounds at its feet, a serene, enormous lilac tree rises.

Each social stage brings to literature its own mode of expression, in such fashion that the history of peoples could be told in the various phases of literature, with greater truth than in chronicles and annals. There can be no contradictions in Nature. The same human aspiration to find a perfect type of charm and beauty in love, during this existence, and in the unknown after death, shows that in the total life we must rejoicingly fit together the elements which in the portion of life we presently traverse seem disunited and hostile. A literature that would announce and spread the final, happy concert of apparent contradictions; a literature that, as a spontaneous counsel and instruction from Nature would proclaim in a superior peace the oneness of the dogmas and rival passions that in the elemental state of peoples divide and plunge them into bloody conflict; a literature that would inculcate in the timid spirit of men such a deep-rooted conviction of justice and definitive beauty that the privations and sordidness of existence will not discourage or embitter them; such a literature will not only reveal a social status closer to perfection than any known, but also, felicitously joining reason to grace, will provide Humanity, eager for marvels and poetry, with the religion it has been confusedly awaiting ever since it realized the hollowness and insufficiency of its old creeds.

Who is so ignorant as to maintain that poetry is not indispensable to the people of the earth? There are persons of such mental myopia that they believe a fruit is finished after the rind. Poetry, which unites or severs, which fortifies or anguishes, which lifts up the souls or casts them down, which gives men faith and comfort or takes them away, is more necessary to peoples than industry itself, since the latter bestows the means for subsisting, while poetry gives them desire and strength for life. Where would a society go that had lost the habit of thinking confidently about the meaning and scope of its acts? The best among them, those whom Nature has anointed with the holy desire for the future, would lose, in a sorrowful and silent annihilation, all incentive to surmount human ugliness; and the masses, the vulgar, the people of appetites, the ordinary, would procreate, without sanctity, hollow children; and would raise to essential functions those which ought to serve as mere instruments. With the bustle of an always incomplete prosperity they would bemuse the irremediable melancholy of the soul, which takes pleasure only in beauty and sublimity.

Other considerations aside, freedom should be blessed, because its enjoyment inspires in modern man—who before its appearance was deprived of the calm, stimulation, and poetry of existence—the supreme peace and religious well-being that the world order produces in those who live in it with the pride and serenity of their free will. Look to the mountains, O poets whose puerile tears dampen deserted altars!

You thought religion lost because it was changing form over your heads. Arise, for you are the priests! Freedom is the definitive religion. And the poetry of freedom is the new form of worship. Such poetry calms and beautifies the present, deduces and illumines the future, explains the ineffable purpose and seductive goodness of the universe.

Listen to what this industrious, satisfied people is singing; listen to Walt Whitman. His exercise of himself raises him into majesty, his tolerance into justice, his sense of order into happiness. He who lives in an autocratic creed is an oyster in its shell, seeing only the prison that enfolds it, and believing, in the darkness, that this is the world. Freedom lends wings to the oyster. And that which, heard from inside the shell, seemed a portentous strife, becomes, in the light of day, the natural movement of fluids in the energetic pulse of the world.

The world, to Walt Whitman, was always as it is today. It suffices that a thing exists for its existence to be justified, and when it should exist no longer, it will cease to exist. That which exists no longer, that which is not seen, is proved by that which does exist and is seen; for everything is in the whole, one thing explaining the other; and when that which is now ceases to be, it will be proved in its turn by that which comes later. The infinitesimal collaborates toward the infinite, and every thing is in its place: a tortoise, an ox, birds, "wing'd purposes." It is just as fortunate to die as to be born, for the dead are alive; "No array of terms can say how much I am at peace about God and about death." He laughs at what they call dissolution, and he knows the amplitude of time. He accepts time absolutely. All is contained in his person; all of him is in everything else; where one degrades himself, Whitman degrades himself; he is the tide, the ebb and the flow; how shall he not be proud of himself, since he feels he is a live and intelligent part of Nature? What does it matter to him if he returns to the bosom whence he came

APPENDIX I

and, in the cool, moist earth, be converted into a useful
plant, a beautiful flower? He will nourish men, after hav-
ing loved them. His duty is to create; the atom that creates
is of divine essence; the act in which one creates is exqui-
site and sacred. Convinced of the identity of the universe,
he intones the "Song of Myself." Out of all things he
weaves the song of himself: of the creeds that struggle
and pass, of man who procreates and labors, of the ani-
mals that help him—Ah, of the animals! "Not one kneels
to another," nor his superior to any other, nor complains.
He sees himself as heir to the world.

Nothing is strange to him, and he takes all into account:
the creeping snail, the ox that looks at him with its mys-
terious eyes, the priest who defends a part of the truth as
though it were the whole truth. Man should open his arms
and clasp all things to his heart, virtue the same as crime,
dirtiness the same as cleanliness, ignorance the same as
wisdom. He should fuse all things in his heart, as in a
furnace; he should let his white beard fall over all things.
But—mark this well!—"We have had ducking and de-
precation about enough." He rebukes the incredulous, the
sophists, the garrulous; let them procreate instead of
quarreling, and they will add something to the world!
Believe with the same respect as a pious woman who
kisses the altar steps!

He belongs to all castes, creeds, and professions, and in
all of them finds justice and poetry. He gauges religions
without anger, but he thinks the perfect religion is in Na-
ture. Religion and life are in Nature. If there is a sick
man, "Go," he says to the physician and the priest; "I
will stay with him. I will open the windows, I will love
him, I will speak softly to him. You shall see how he re-
covers; you are the words and the herbs, but I can do more
than you, for I am love." The Creator is the "Lover divine

63

and perfect Comrade"; men are "cameradoes"; and the more they love and believe, the more they are worth, although anything that keeps its place and its time is worth as much as any other. But let all see the world for themselves, since he, Walt Whitman, who feels within himself the whole of the world since its creation, knows by what the sun and open air teach him that a sunrise reveals more than the best book. He thinks of orbs, and desires women, feels himself possessed by universal, frenzied love. From scenes of creation and the trades of men he hears rising a concert of music to overflow him with joy, and when he looks into a river at the moment when shops are closing and the setting sun ignites the water, he feels he has an appointment with the Creator; he recognizes that man is definitely good and from his head, reflected in the current, he sees spokes of light diverge.

But what can give an idea of his vast, burning love? This man loves the world with the fire of Sappho. He sees the world as a gigantic bed. The bed is an altar to him. "I will prove illustrious," he says, "the words and ideas that men have prostituted with their stealth and false shame; I sing and consecrate what Egypt consecrated." One of the sources of his originality is the Herculean force with which he prostrates ideas, as though he were going to rape them, when in reality he is only going to give them a kiss, with the fervor of a saint. Another source is the material, brutal, fleshly form with which he expresses his most delicate idealities. Such language has seemed lascivious to some who are incapable of understanding its grandeur. There have been imbeciles who, with the prudishness of nasty minded school boys, when in "Calamus" he celebrates love among friends with the warmest images in the human tongue, have felt they saw a return to the ignoble yearning of Virgil for Cebetes and of Horace for

APPENDIX I

Gyges and Lyciscus. And when in "Children of Adam" he sings the divine sin, in pictures that dim the most glowing of the "Song of Solomon," he trembles, he shrinks, he pours himself out and expands, he goes mad with pride and satisfied virility; he recalls the god of the Amazon who passes over forests and rivers scattering seeds of life: "My duty is to Create!" "I sing the body electric," Whitman says in "Children of Adam"; and one should first read in Hebrew the patriarchal genealogies of Genesis; one should follow the naked, carnivorous bands of the first men through the trackless jungles, in order to find an appropriate resemblance to the enumeration, full of Satanic might, where like a famished hero licking bloodstained lips he describes the pertinencies of the female body. You say this man is brutal? Listen to this poem which, like many of his, has only two lines:

"Beautiful Women"

Women sit or move to and fro, some old, some young,
The young are beautiful—but the old are more beautiful than the young.

And this one:

"Mother and Babe"

I see the sleeping babe ʼnestling the breast of its mother,
The sleeping mother and babe—hush'd, I study them long and long.

He foresees that just as virility and gentleness already combine to a high degree in men of superior character, so the two energies which have had to become separated from each other in order to continue the task of Creation must come together again, with a solemnity and joy worthy of the universe, in that delightful peace on which life will rest.

65

If he walks into the grass, he says that the grass caresses him, that he "already feels its joints move," and the most restless novice would not find such fiery words to describe the joy of his body, which he looks upon as part of his soul, when it feels itself embraced by the sea. All living things love him: earth, night, and sea love him: "You sea . . . Dash me with amorous wet." He savors the air. He gives himself to the atmosphere like a tremulous bridegroom. He wants doors with no lock and bodies in their natural beauty; he believes he sanctifies all he touches or that touches him, and he finds virtue in all corporeality; he is

Walt Whitman, a kosmos, of Manhattan the son,
Turbulent, fleshy, sensual, eating, drinking and breeding,
. . . no stander above men and women or apart from them.

He depicts truth as a frantic lover who invades his body and, eager to possess him, frees him from his garments. But in the clarity of midnight the soul, free of occupations and books, emerges integral, silent, and meditative from a nobly spent day, and reflects on the themes that please it most: on night, dreams, and death; on the song of the universal for the benefit of the common man; on how it is very sweet "to die advancing on" and to fall at the foot of a primitive tree, holding the ax in one's hands, stung by the last serpent in the woods.

Imagine, then, what a new strange effect this language, charged with splendid animality, must produce when it extols the passion that will unite men. In one poem of "Calamus" the poet brings together the delights he owes Nature and Country; but he finds that only the ocean waves are worthy to chorus by moonlight his joy at seeing by his side, asleep, the friend whom he loves. He loves the humble, the fallen, the wounded, even the evildoer. He does not scorn the great, for to him only the useful are great. He puts his arm around the shoulders of teamsters, sailors, plowmen. He hunts and fishes with them, and at harvest time climbs with them atop of the loaded wagon. More beautiful to him than a triumphant emperor is a brawny Negro who standing on the shaft behind his Percherons drives his dray calmly along busy Broadway. He understands all virtues, wins all prizes, works at all trades, suffers all pains, feels a heroic pleasure when he stops on the threshold of a smithy and sees that the young men, stripped to the waist, swing their hammers overhand and each one hits in turn. He is the slave, the prisoner, he who fights, who falls, the beggar. When a slave comes to his door harried and covered with sweat, he fills a tub for him, has him sit at his table; in the corner he has his firelock loaded to defend him; if anyone comes to attack the slave he will kill the pursuer and come back to sit at his table, as though he had killed a snake.

Walt Whitman, then, is satisfied; what pride can sting him when he knows we end up as a blade of grass or a flower? What pride does a carnation have, or a leaf of salvia, or a honeysuckle vine? Why should he not look on human grief with equanimity when he knows that above all this there is an eternal being for whom there waits a happy immersion in Nature? What haste shall spur him when he believes all is where it belongs, and the will of one man cannot change the path of the world? He suffers, yes, he suffers; but he considers minor and passing the part of him that suffers, and above toil and misery he feels there is another part that cannot suffer, for it knows universal greatness. It is enough for him to be as he is; and he watches, impassive and cheerful, the flow of his life, whether in silence or in acclamation. With a single blow he knocks aside romantic lamentation, a useless excrescence. "Not asking the sky to come down to my good will!" And what majesty there is in the phrase where he says that he loves animals because "they do not sweat and whine about their condition." The truth is that there are already too many who would make cowards of us. There is a pressing need to see what the world is like, in order not to make ants into mountains. Give men strength instead of taking from them with lamentations the little that pain has left them. Do the ulcerated go through the streets showing their sores? Neither doubt nor science disturbs him. "To you the first honours," he says to the scientists. "Your facts are useful, and yet they are not my dwelling, I but enter by them to an area of my dwelling." "How beggarly appear arguments before a defiant deed!" "Lo! keen-eyed towering science . . . Yet again, lo! the soul, above all science." But where his philosophy has completely mastered hate, as the wise men command, is in the phrase—not untinged with the melancholy of defeat— with which he uproots all envy: "Why should I envy," he says, "any brother of mine who does what I cannot do?" "He that by me spreads a wider breast than my own proves the width of my own." "Let the sun penetrate the Earth, until it is all clear, sweet light, like my blood. Let joy be universal. I sing the eternity of existence, the joy of our life, and the implacable beauty of the universe. I wear calfskin shoes, a wide collar, and a cane cut from a branch!"

All this he utters in apocalyptic phrases. Rhymes, stresses? Oh, no! His rhythm lies in the stanzas which, in the midst of an apparent chaos of overlying and convulsed sentences, are nevertheless linked by a wise method of composition that distributes the ideas in large musical groups, as the natural poetic form of a people who do not build stone by stone but with huge boulders.

APPENDIX I

Walt Whitman's language, entirely different from that which poets have used till now, corresponds in its extravagance and power to his cyclic poetry and to the new humanity congregated on a fertile continent under auspices of such magnitude as not to be contained in ditties or coy lyrics. It is no longer a matter of clandestine amours or of courtly ladies trading old gallants for new, or of sterile complaints by those who lack the energy to master life, or of discretion suitable to cowards. Nor is it a matter of jingles and boudoir sighings, but of the birth of an era, the dawn of a definitive religion and of the renewal of mankind. It is a matter of a faith to replace the dead one, and it is revealed in the radiance of a redeemed man's proud peace; it is a matter of writing the holy books for a people who, as the old world declines, join all the virgin power of liberty with the udders and Cyclopean pomp of wild Nature. It is a matter of reflecting in words the noise of settling multitudes, of toiling cities, of tamed oceans and enslaved rivers. Should Walt Whitman then match rhymes and put into mild couplets these mountains of merchandise, forests of thorns, towns full of ships, battles where millions of men lay down their lives to insure the laws, and a sun that holds sway over all and pours its limpid fire into the vast landscape?

Oh, no! Walt Whitman speaks in Biblical verses; without apparent music, although after hearing them for a short time one realizes that these sounds ring like the earth's mighty shell when it is trodden by triumphant armies, barefoot and glorious. At times Whitman's language is like the front of a butcher shop hung with beef carcasses; at others it resembles the song of patriarchs seated in a circle, with the sadness of the world at the time of day when smoke loses itself among the clouds. Sometimes it sounds like an abrupt kiss, like a ravishment, like the cracking of leather as it dries in the sun. But never does his utterance lose its rhythmical, wavy motion. He himself tells how he speaks in "prophetical screams." These, he says, are "a few indicative words of the future." That is what his poetry is, an index finger; a sense of the universal pervades the book and gives it, within the surface confusion, a grandiose regularity; but his sentences—disjointed, flagellant, incomplete, unconnected—emit rather than express. "I send out my imaginings over the hoary mountains"; "Earth . . . Say, old top-knot, what do you want?" "I sound my barbaric yawp over the roofs of the world."

He is not the kind to set in motion a beggarly thought to stumble and creep along under the outward opulence of its regal dress. He is not one to puff up hummingbirds to resemble eagles; he showers down eagles every time he opens his hand, as a sower broadcasts seeds. One line may have five syllables, the following forty, and the one after that ten. He does not strain comparisons; as a matter of fact, he does not compare at all but says what he sees or remembers with a graphic, incisive complement and, being a confident master of the total impression he is ready to create, he uses his art, concealing it completely, to reproduce the elements of his picture with the same disarray in which he observed them in Nature. Although he may wander off, he does not make discords, for this is the way the mind wanders—without order or bondage—from a subject to its analogues; but then, as though he had only loosened the reins without dropping them altogether, he draws them suddenly tight and with a masterful hand keeps close control over his restive team, while his lines gallop along, swallowing up distances with each movement. Sometimes they whinny eagerly like stud stallions; at other times, white and lathered, they set their hoofs on the clouds; and at still others, dark and daring, they plunge inside the earth, and for a long while we hear the rumbling noise. Whitman sketches, but you would say he sketches with fire. In five lines he groups, like a sheaf of freshly gnawed bones, all the horrors of war. An adverb is enough to expand or contract a phrase, and an adjective to sublimate it. His method has to be great, since its effect is; but it might be thought that he proceeds without any method whatsoever, especially in his use of words, which he mixes with unheard-of audacity, putting the august and almost divine side by side with those which are considered less appropriate and polite. Certain pictures he does not paint with epithets—which with him are always lively and profound—but with sounds, which he assembles and disperses with consummate skill; thus, with a succession of procedures, maintaining interest, which the monotony of an exclusive mode would have jeopardized. Through repetitions he draws out melancholia like the savages. His caesura, unexpected and run-on, he changes ceaselessly and without conforming to any rule, although an intelligent arrangement can be detected in its evolutions, pauses, and trills. He finds that accumulation is the best way to describe, and his reasoning never assumes the pedestrian form of argumentation or the high-sounding form of oratory, but instead uses the mystery of suggestion, the fervor of certainty, and the flaming word of prophecy.

At every step of the way we find words from our Spanish: *viva, camarada, libertad, americanos*. But what could better depict his character than the French words which, in visible ecstasy and as though to expand their meaning, he embeds in his poems: *ami, exalté, accoucheur, nonchalant, ensemble? Ensemble*, especially, charms him, for he sees in it the heaven of the life of the peoples and the worlds. From the Italian he has taken one word: *bravura!*

Thus, honoring muscle and boldness; inviting passers-by to put their hands on him without fear; hearing the song of things, with his palms upturned to the air; surprising and proclaiming with delight gigantic fecundities; gathering up in epic verse, seeds, battles, and orbs; showing astounded generations the radiant hives of men who spread out on American valleys and peaks, and brush with their wings the hem of vigilant Liberty's gown; shepherding the friendly centuries toward the sheltering bay of eternal calm; thus, while upon rustic tablecloths his friends serve him the first catch of Spring fish washed down with champagne, Walt Whitman awaits the happy hour when the material substance shall separate from him, after having revealed to the world a truthful, sonorous, and loving man, and when, given over to the purifying air, he will germinate and embalm its waves, "disembodied, triumphant, dead!"

APPENDIX II

NOTES ON THE POETS AND THE POEMS

Jorge Luis Borges
(Argentina, 1899)

The greatness of Borges as a writer centers around his short essays and narratives, quintessential distillations of metaphysical games and paradoxes. As André Maurois has noted in the preface to the English edition of *Labyrinths*, the art of Borges may well be defined with his own description of the imaginary metaphysicians of Tlön: "They seek neither truth nor likelihood; they seek astonishment. They think metaphysics is a branch of the literature of fantasy." However, Borges initiated his literary career as a poet (*Fervor de Buenos Aires*, 1923) and as one of the founders of a poetic movement called *"ultraísmo,"* which aimed at the reduction of the poem to what was considered its essential element: the metaphor. Borges still continues to publish verse, periodically compiled in ever-growing editions of his *Obra poética*. It is a poetry of sober nostalgia, and as perplexing, at times, as his short stories. In the opening page of his *Obra poética*, Borges modestly qualifies his poetry with the following quotation from Robert Louis Stevenson: "I do not set up to be a poet. Only an all-round literary man: a man who talks, not one who sings . . . Excuse this apology; but I don't like to come before people who have a note of song, and let it be supposed I do not know the difference."

Borges has written two suggestive essays on Whitman, "El otro Whitman" and "Una nota sobre Whitman" (*Dis-*

73

cusión, 1957), and has often expressed his long-standing admiration for the North American poet.[1] The poem "Camden, 1892" appears in the 1966 edition of his *Obra poética*, along with other poems to literary figures, such as Homer, Milton, Cervantes, Emerson, Poe and Heine. With his pantheistic perspective of man, history, and the Universe, Borges seems to identify the mortal destiny of these literary figures with his own, as well as that of the reader. Such is the theme of the poem, reminiscent of Walt Whitman for its title, "A quien está leyéndome" ("To whoever is reading me," p. 265), in which Borges reminds the reader of his own transitoriness, but the reader seems to be Borges himself.

A number of Borges' works are now available in English translation: *Ficciones* (Grove Press, 1962) and *Labyrinths* (New Directions, 1962) contain selected prose writings; *Dreamtigers* (University of Texas Press, 1964) is a translation of *El hacedor*, which contains prose and poetry; *Other Inquisitions* (University of Texas Press, 1965) is an anthology of essays; and *A Personal Anthology* (Grove Press, 1967) offers the author's choice of his own prose and poetry.

LEÓN FELIPE
(Spain, 1884–Mexico, 1968)

León Felipe's full name was León Felipe Camino Galicia. From 1920, when he published his first book of poetry, *Versos y oraciones del caminante*, he was a wandering poet, with periods of residence in Fernando Poo Islands

[1] See my article "Borges y Whitman," *Hispania*, vol. L, no. 1, (March, 1967), pp. 49–53. The essay "Note on Whitman" appears in *Other Inquisitions, 1937–1952*, pp. 66–72.

(off the African coast), in Mexico, in New York City, where he attended Columbia University, and in Panama. He made extensive tours of Latin America reading his poetry, and innumerable Atlantic crossings.

His poetry is simple, almost plain, foreshadowing the Neruda of *Elementary Odes* in both style and its appeal to human fraternity: Walt Whitman is their common root. The poem in this collection is an excerpt from a verse prologue that León Felipe wrote for his controversial translation, or paraphrasis, of Walt Whitman's "Song of Myself" (Buenos Aires: Losada, 1941). Other works include *Drop a Star* (1930), *Español del exodo y del llanto* (1939), *Ganarás la luz . . .* (1943), *El ciervo* (1958), and translations from Shakespeare. León Felipe's complete works (*Obras completas*) were published by Losada (Buenos Aires, in 1963), as one volume in a series devoted to the complete works of the most outstanding contemporary poets in Spanish.

LEOPOLDO LUGONES
(Argentina, 1874–1938)

Lugones' literary career reveals great versatility. It includes history and fiction as well as poetry. Especially noteworthy are some of his short stories (*Las fuerzas extrañas*, 1906), reminiscent of Frank Kafka and forerunner of Borges. His poetry includes several volumes of the most varied kinds. In the beginning (*Las montañas del oro*, 1897, *Crepúsculos del jardín*, 1905, and *Lunario sentimental*, 1909) it is hermetic and Symbolist, but it can also be patriotic (*Odas seculares*, 1910), romantic (*El libro fiel*, 1912), or popular (*Libro de los paisajes*, 1917, and *Romances de Río Seco*, 1938). It reflects the influence of

APPENDIX II

Hugo, Poe, Baudelaire, Verlaine, and Mallarmé, as well as Rubén Darío and the Uruguayan Julio Herrera y Reissig. It is a poetry which, although lacking in lyrical depth, reveals a great mastery of poetic language. This is, in general, characteristic of many Spanish American poets of the *modernista* movement headed by Rubén Darío, the Nicaraguan poet, whom Lugones met in Buenos Aires in 1896, when the former was at the climax of his career, devoted to the renovation of Spanish poetry under the influence of the French Schools.

In 1897, Lugones published his first book, *Las montañas del oro*. The work was written under the spell of Victor Hugo, but it revealed fresh talent and originality. In this respect, Jorge Luis Borges, in his book on Lugones, expresses the following opinion:

All through the book, the presence of Hugo is evident. This influence is one for which Lugones has been criticized many times. There is much to be said against this. To imitate Hugo is not easy. To imitate him without lapsing into mere grandiloquence and without allowing the tone to weaken is a difficult task, even for Hugo himself; Lugones, however, accomplishes this with ease.[2]

The introduction to the book, a long poem in Alexandrine couplets from which I present only an excerpt, is a eulogy on the mission of the Poet as the great revealer and avant-garde of humanity, an illustrious figure in History's procession, a hero whose own greatness isolates him from the rest of mankind—as a leader is alone in the midst of his followers. In a way, the whole poem is an attempt on the part of Lugones to define his own position as a poet in relation to humanity, the New World, and the Cosmos. Besides the influence of Hugo (e.g., "Les mages"), the influence of Walt Whitman can also be detected in certain

[2] Jorge Luis Borges, *Leopoldo Lugones* (Buenos Aires: Ed. Troquel, 1955), p. 27.

parts of the poem, as Fernando Alegría has indicated.[3]
Lugones pays homage to the North American poet by in-
cluding him in his selection of the four greatest poets of
humanity, with Hugo, Dante, and Homer.

RUBÉN DARÍO
(Nicaragua, 1867–1916)

In Spanish American poetry, Rubén Darío represents
what Edgar Allen Poe does in North American poetry. The
similarity lies not in the characteristics of their work
but in the fact that each was the first poet from his nation
to be acclaimed and accepted as an equal on the Con-
tinent, and even exert his influence on the literature of
the Old World. Rubén Darío lived in Paris during a sig-
nificant part of his life, and could be more readily identi-
fied with the City of Lights than with his native Nicaragua.
The French influence is strongly felt in this poet's work,
and it is through this influence, especially that of the
Parnasians and Symbolists, that Rubén Darío effected
the renovation of Spanish poetry, both in Spain and
Spanish America, at the turn of the century. This was the
movement known as *modernismo*, which placed prime
importance on the musical qualities of the language and
emphasized aristocracy and exquisite sensibility in art
and life.

There was a moment in Darío's youth when, perhaps by
way of the essay on Walt Whitman by José Martí, the
ideals of Whitman affected the thought and sensibility
of Darío. This can be discerned in the following profession
of faith:

[3] *Walt Whitman en Hispanoamérica*, p. 269.

77

APPENDIX II

I believe that the sacred cult of Nature, of a great and universal God, of boundless charity, ought to be the cult of all poets; and the Cosmos, the object of sublime love . . . Before the proud statue of Schopenhauer, I would place the tall and radiant statue of the luminous Hegel. Even more, above all the sad and lifeless thinkers, in the midst of ancient and modern philosophical darkness, I see, majestic and prophetic, the image of a venerable old man who is still living, who has appeared in the regions of freedom and tomorrow, and whose voice begins to resound everywhere because he is today the world's first poet, and he loves humanity with boundless love, like Hugo, more so than Shelley or pale Dostoievsky: I am speaking of Whitman, the Yankee pontiff with the white beard.[4]

As we can see, however, Darío's professed doctrine of universal love had more of the abstract and metaphysical than of the immediate and sensuous conception of Walt Whitman, and was later abandoned by Darío for the sake of artistic excellence. Darío continued to admire Whitman but not what he represented, as in the following passage in which Darío refers to his own poetic and intellectual development:

However, abominating democracy, deadly to poets—be its admirers even as Walt Whitman—I leaned towards the past, to the ancient myths and the splendid histories, thus incurring the censorship of the nearsighted.[5]

Or in the preface to one of his books:

(If there is any poetry in our America, it is in the old things: In Palenke and Utatlán, in the legendary Indian and the sensual and refined Inca, and in the great Moctezuma of the golden chair. The rest is yours, democrat Walt Whitman).[6]

[4] Translation of a passage from *Obras desconocidas de Darío*, ed. Raúl Castro Silva (Santiago: Prensas Universitarias de Chile, 1934), pp. 249–50; quoted by Alegría, *Walt Whitman en Hispanoamérica*, p. 252.

[5] Translation of a passage from *Historia de mis libros*, in *Obras completas* (Madrid: A. Aguado, 1950), vol. I, p. 206.

[6] Ibid., vol. V, p. 763.

APPENDIX II

Darío's sonnet to Walt Whitman appeared in 1890 as one of several "Medallones," in the second edition of one of his early books, *Azul*. These, as described by the poet himself, were "lyrical portraits; medallions of poets who were some of my admirations of the day: Leconte de Lisle, Catulle Méndes, the Yankee Walt Whitman, the Cuban J. J. Palma, the Mexican Salvador Díaz Mirón." In it, we already find the *modernista* conception of the role of the Poet, which, in certain respects, coincided with Whitman's own conception of the poet as interpreter and chanter of the Universe, endowed with a divine inspiration which shines forth, not only in the tone and majesty of his verse, but also in his physical appearance, surrounding him with a mystic aureole. In his portrait, Darío draws not merely a semblance of Walt Whitman, but of Whitman as the Poet *par excellence*. This should explain his choice of images to draw a universal and majestic figure, rather than a more personal and individualized one.

EZEQUIEL MARTÍNEZ ESTRADA
(Argentina, 1895–1965)

Like some of his Argentine compatriots, such as Echeverría and Borges, Ezequiel Martínez Estrada began his literary career as a poet, then abruptly interrupted it to become a brilliant essayist. His poetry belongs to his youth. His last volume of poetry during this period, *Humoresca* (1929), merited the Argentine "Premio Nacional de Letras." It includes the poem to Walt Whitman, in a section titled "Tres estrellas de la osa menor," along with poems to Emerson and Poe. Jorge Luis Borges, in the prologue to *Antología poética argentina* (Buenos Aires: Ed. Sudamericana, 1941), in which the poem to Walt Whitman is included, referred to Martínez Estrada as "nuestro mejor poeta contemporáneo." However, it was his work as an essayist (*Radiografía de la Pampa*, 1933) and critic (*Muerte y transfiguración de Martín Fierro*, 1948) that won him recognition outside his country. His basic preoccupation, obvious in the poem to Whitman, was more social than lyrical. This is not unusual in Spanish-American letters, where there is a certain disregard for the European literary obsession with the self.

In 1959, he published another volume of verse, *Coplas de ciego*, reminiscent of some of the cerebral *coplas* of Antonio Machado. He was a professor at the School of Political Science at the University of Mexico in 1960, and in 1962 he published his last important book, *Diferencias y semejanzas entre los países de la América Latina*, and went to Cuba as a supporter of the Castro Revolution.

ALFREDO CARDONA PEÑA
(Costa Rica, 1917)

Cardona Peña lives in Mexico City, where he has lived most of his life. His poetic production, in the ultra-modern and surrealist vein of García Lorca and Neruda, has been extensive. His *Poemas numerales (1944–1948)*, won the "Premio Centroamericano" in 1948. His poem to Walt Whitman, in *Los jardines amantes* (1952), is included in a section titled "Poemas a poemas," devoted to poetic homages to some of his favorite literary figures, such as Sor Juana, the Mexican poet-nun of the XVII century, the Peruvian César Vallejo, Lautréamont, Balzac, the Colombian Porfirio Barba-Jacob, and Neruda. What do they have in common, one may wonder. Perhaps a certain *barroquism?*—or is it their social-mindedness? Traditionally, Spanish-American letters have followed two alternative courses: loss of self in social literature, or loss of self in linguistic artistry. Often the two come together, and this is the path that Cardona Peña has tried to follow.

FEDERICO GARCÍA LORCA
(Spain, 1898–1936)

Federico García Lorca, Antonio Machado, and Juan Ramón Jiménez are the three preeminent twentieth-century Spanish poets. García Lorca's early career, between music and poetry, resulted in the musical poetry with a backdrop of gypsy life of *Primer romancero gitano* (1928) and *Poema del cante jondo* (1931), and culminated in his masterpiece of poetic elegy, *Llanto por Ignacio Sánchez Mejía* (1935), undoubtedly one of the finest pieces of elegiac poetry in any language, within the magnificent tradition of that other Spanish master of elegy, Jorge Manrique.

García Lorca's "Ode to Walt Whitman," along with most of the poems of *Poeta en Nueva York*, was written in 1929, during García Lorca's Columbia University period. *Poeta en Nueva York* is a surrealistic work of a deeply symbolic nature (in discussing it, critics always feel compelled to mention García Lorca's friendship with Salvador Dalí). Considered within its framework, the "Ode to Walt Whitman" offers a synthesis, climax, and solution to the underlying theme of the book. New York symbolizes not only the evils of civiliza-

tion, or of a particular form of civilization that dehuman-
izes man, but, in a broader sense, the "inhuman" aspect
of man, which finds expression and appears concentrated
in this city of filth and perversion. The poetic nature of
man, his capacity to dream, and his love of beauty are
conspicuously absent. In order to maintain his faith in the
spiritual nature of man, the poet evokes the image of Walt
Whitman. His portrait, then, obeys the necessity of erect-
ing him as a symbol of purity, of spiritual nobility and
silent heroism.

The "Ode to Walt Whitman" was first published in a
limited edition in Mexico City (Alcancía) in 1933. In 1939,
it was translated into English by Stephen Spender and
J. L. Gili, for *The Dolphin*, and is included in their edition
of *Selected Poems of Federico García Lorca* (1947). The
bilingual edition of *Poet in New York* (1940), by Rolfe
Humphries, claimed to offer the "Ode to Walt Whitman"
complete for the first time both in English or Spanish. A
new bilingual edition of *Poet in New York,* by Ben Bellit,
appeared in 1955. Although I present a new translation of
the "Ode to Walt Whitman," mine is, of course, indebted
to these previous ones.

PEDRO MIR
(Dominican Republic, 1912)

Part of Pedro Mir's work published before his exile
from the island during the Trujillo regime appeared
in anthologies such as *Antología poética dominicana*
(1951), by Pedro René Contín Aybar, and *Nueva poesía
dominicana* (1953), by Antonio Fernández Spencer. Some
of these previously published poems were reprinted in

APPENDIX II

Santo Domingo after the fall of Trujillo under the title *Hay un país en el mundo y 6 momentos de esperanza* (Ediciones Claridad, 1962). His poetry is deeply concerned with social injustice and political oppression, and has a clearly socialistic tendency. *Contracanto a Walt Whitman: Canto a nosotros mismos* is a long poem which traces with epic images the growth of the United States and American democracy on the basis of an exalted notion of self. Later on, however, this independent self is swallowed and imprisoned by the growth of selfishness, expressed in the growth of Banks, Trusts, and Monopolies. The country expands and exploits the Latin American nations. Now, as a solution, comes the hour of the Countersong to Walt Whitman, not the "Song of Myself," but the "Song of Ourselves," the song of the collective action of a laboring humanity. The poem consists of seventeen sections, from which I have selected a few, trying to preserve the tone and unity of the original. It was first published in Guatemala, in 1952, by a poetry group called Saker-Ti.

PABLO NERUDA
(Chile, 1904)

Neruda's poetry has been extensive, and like that of Lugones, varied, both in topic and style. It runs the gamut from the *modernista* tendency of his first important book, *Crepusculario* (1932), through the modernistic romanticism of *20 poemas de amor y una canción de desesperada* (1924), and the obscure and hermetic, desolate poetry of *Residencia en la tierra* (poems from 1925 to 1935), to the political poetry of *Canto general* (1950) and the simple lyric of the *Odas elementales* and more recent books. It has been translated into many languages. In English, we have *Residence on Earth and other Poems* (1946); long excerpts from "Summits of Macchu Picchu," from *Canto general,* included in *The World's Best* (1950), edited by Whit Burnett; and more recently, *Twenty Poems* (The Sixties Press, 1967). Twenty-one of the over one hundred and eighty of his "Elementary Odes," which appeared in three volumes: *Odas elementales* (1954), *Nuevas odas elementales* (1956), and *Tercer libro de las odas* (1957) (a fourth volume of Odes was *Navegaciones y regresos,* 1959)—were published in translation under the title *The Elementary Odes of Pablo Neruda,* by Carlos Lozano, in 1961. The "Ode to Walt Whitman" is included among these, and my own translation is naturally indebted to it.

Neruda is the Spanish-American poet who shows the closest affinity with Walt Whitman. Fernando Alegría accurately traced the relationship between Neruda and Whitman up to the former's *Canto general.* The subsequent publication of the *Odas elementales* continues this tendency, the result of a basic attitude shared by the two poets: that of an erotic response to, and interaction with, the everyday world. The introduction to the *Odas*—a poem titled "El hombre invisible," referring to the role of the poet who absorbs everything that surrounds him and makes it part of himself (as in Whitman's "There was a child went forth every day")—is a statement of a poetic creed which, although it may have a socialistic meaning, or perhaps because it does, is directly related to Whitman:

> I want
> everyone to live

in my life
and sing in my song,[7]

writes Neruda, placing himself in a perspective similar
to the one previously assumed by Walt Whitman:

Give me for my life
all the lives,
give me all the sorrows
of the world.
I shall transform them
into hope.
Give me
all the joys.
... ...
I have to retell them,
give me
the everyday
struggles
because they are my song,
thus we shall walk together
rubbing elbows,
with every man,
my song brings them together:
the song of the invisible man
who sings with every man.[8]

A similar theme is repeated in the "Ode to the Simple
Man":

You are life,
you are transparent
like water,
and so am I,
such is my task:
To be transparent.
Each day
I learn,

[7] Translation of an excerpt from *Odas elementales*, in *Obras
completas* (Buenos Aires: Losada, 1962), p. 938.
[8] Ibid., p. 941.

each day I comb my hair
thinking how you think,
I walk
as you walk
and eat as you do.
I hold my love in my arms
as you your sweetheart,
and then,
when all is proven,
when we are equal,
I write,
I write with your life and mine,
with your love and mine,
with all our sorrows.[9]

Neruda's homage to Walt Whitman, therefore, emerges naturally from his poetic attitude. His "Ode to Walt Whitman" is a recognition to the emotive affinities of man, and what Neruda says of Walt Whitman:

To every corner of your town
a verse
of yours arrived for a visit,
and it was like a piece
of clean body,
the verse that arrived,

he would probably like to say of himself, as in these words from the introduction to his *Obras completas:*

It should not be surprising, then, that I have tried to repay human brotherhood with something balsamic, fragrant and earthy. Just as I once left that pine-cone there, I have laid my words at the door of many unknown people, of many prisoners, of many lonely ones, of many who suffer persecutions.[10]

In an interview by Robert Bly, which took place in New York, June 12, 1966, Neruda expressed the following opinions about Whitman:

[9] Ibid., p. 1009.
[10] Ibid., p. 30.

APPENDIX II

... Whitman was a great teacher. Because what is Whitman? He was not only intensely conscious, but he was open-eyed! He had tremendous eyes to see everything—he taught us to see things. He was our poet.

(Question:) *Whitman has clearly had much more influence on the Spanish poets than on the North American poets. Why didn't the North American poets understand him? Was it because of the influence of England?*

Perhaps, perhaps the intellectualist influence of England. Also many of the American poets just following Eliot thought that Whitman was too rustic, too primitive. But he is not so simple—Whitman—he's a complicated man and the best of him is when he is most complicated. He had eyes opened to the world and he taught us about poetry and many other things. We have loved him very much. Eliot never had much influence with us. He's too intellectual perhaps, we are too primitive. And then everyone has to choose a road—a refined and intellectual way, or a more brotherly, general way, trying to embrace the world around you, to discover the new world.[11]

[11] Printed in *Twenty Poems of Pablo Neruda*, translated by James Wright and Robert Bly (Madison, Minn.: The Sixties Press, 1967), p. 103.